Contents

Introduction	1
1 UnderstandingProcrastination:Defining the Enemy	8
Definition Causes of Procrastination	9
Effects of Procrastination The	10
Psychology Behind Procrastination	12
	14
2 BreakingDownTasks:DivideandConquer	17
The Art of Breaking Down Tasks	18
Why Breaking Down Tasks Works	18
Practical Methods for Breaking Down Tasks	19
Overcoming Common Challenges	21
Tools for Task Breakdown	22
Techniques to Implement Immediately	23
3 SettingClearGoals:AimforSuccess	26
The Power of Goal Setting	27
The Importance of Goal Setting	27
SMART Goals	28
Understanding SMART Goals	28
Crafting Your SMART Goals	30
How is this goal SMART?	32
Overcoming Common Goal-Setting Pitfalls	32
4 PrioritizingTasks:FocusonWhatMatters	35
The Importance of Prioritizing Tasks	36

The Eisenhower Matrix: A Tool for Effective Prioritization	37
Overcoming Common Prioritization Challenges	41
Techniques to Maintain Focus on Priorities	43
5 CreatingaSchedule:PlanYourDay	45
The Benefits of a Structured Schedule	46
Creating an Effective Schedule	47
Overcoming Common Scheduling Challenges	50
6 EliminatingDistractions:MinimizeInterruptions	53
The Cost of Distractions	53
Understanding the Impact of Distractions	54
Identifying Common Distractions	55
Overcoming Common Eliminating Distraction Challenges	56
Strategies for Eliminating Digital Distractions	58
Strategies for Minimizing Environmental Distractions	58
Strategies for Managing Internal Distractions	59
Techniques to Minimize Task Switching	60
Techniques to Sustain Focus and Minimize Interruptions	62
7 BuildingSelf-Discipline:DevelopGoodHabits	64
Understanding Self-Discipline	65
Key Components of Self-Discipline:	65
Strategies for Building Self-Discipline	66
The Importance of Developing Good Habits	67
Developing Good Habits	67
Overcoming Common Self-Discipline Challenges	69
Benefits of Good Habits:	70
8 Overcoming Fear and Anxiety: Face Your Fears	73
Understanding Fear and Anxiety	74

CommonSourcesofFearandAnxiety:	74
TheImpactofFearandAnxietyonProductivity	75
StrategiesforOvercomingFearandAnxiety	75
Overcoming Common Challenges in FacingFears	78
9 Creating a Conducive Work Environment:OptimizeYourSpace	82
TheImportanceofaConduciveWorkEnvironment	82
KeyElementsofaConduciveWorkEnvironment	83
CreatingYourIdealWorkEnvironment	85
Overcoming Common Organizing Workspace Challenges	87
Techniques to Maintain a Conducive Work Environment	90
10GettingAccountability:FindaStudyBuddy	92
ThePowerofAccountability	92
BenefitsofAccountability:	93
FindingYourIdealStudyBuddy	94
EstablishinganEffectiveStudyBuddySystem	95
MaximizingYourStudyBuddyRelationship	97
OvercomingCommonChallenges	98
11 RewardingProgress:CelebrateSmallWins	102
TheImportanceofCelebratingSmallWins	103
Strategies for Identifying and Celebrating SmallWins	104
Overcoming Challenges In Celebrating SmallWins	106
DifferentWaystoCelebrateSmallWins	108
CultivatingaSmallWinsMindset	109
Techniques to Integrate Celebrations into YourRoutine	111
12BuildingResilience:BounceBackfromFailure	113

Understanding Resilience Key Aspects of Resilience: The Link Between Resilience and Procrastination Strategies to Build Resilience Overcoming Common Challenges in Building Resilience Building Resilience in Daily Life 114
114
114
115
117
119

13 Using Technology to Your Advantage: Productivity Tools

122

The Role of Technology in Productivity 123
Essential Productivity Tools 124
Overcoming Common Challenges 128
Integrating Productivity Tools into Your Routine . 129

14 Creating a Morning Routine: Start Your Day Right

133

The Importance of a Morning Routine 134
Elements of an Effective Morning Routine 135
Overcoming Common Challenges 137
Tips for Maintaining Your Morning Routine 138

15 Avoiding Multitasking: Focus on One Thing 141

The Myth of Multitasking 141
Benefits of Focusing on One Task 142
Strategies to Avoid Multitasking and Focus on One Thing 144
Overcoming Common Challenges 145

16 Taking Breaks: Rest and Recharge 149

The Importance of Taking Breaks 150
Types of Breaks 150
Strategies for Effective Breaks 152
Overcoming Guilt and Resistance to Taking Breaks 153

Leveraging Breaks to Combat Specific Types of Procrastination	155
The Role of Extended Breaks	156
17 SeekingHelpWhenNeeded: Don'tBe Afraid to Ask	159
The Importance of Asking for Help	160
Recognizing When You Need Help	160
Overcoming the Fear of Asking for Help	161
Identifying Sources of Help	163
How to Ask for Help Effectively	164
Making the Most of Help Received	166
Building a Support Network	167
18 StayingMotivated:FindYourWhy	170
The Importance of Finding Your Why	170
Types of Motivation:	171
Discovering Your Why	172
Strategies for Staying Motivated	173
Overcoming Motivation Slumps	175
Practical Exercises for Finding and Staying Connected to Your Why	177
19 OvercomingPerfectionism:EmbraceImperfection	179
Understanding Perfectionism The Costs of	180
Perfectionism Strategies for Overcoming	180
Perfectionism Strategies for Overcoming	181
Perfectionism Practical Exercises to Embrace	185
Imperfection	187
20 UsingMindfulness:StayPresentandFocused	190
What is Mindfulness?	191
The Benefits of Mindfulness	191
Techniques for Cultivating Mindfulness	192
Incorporating Mindfulness into Daily Life	194

Overcoming Common Challenges in Mindfulness Practice	195
21 Building a Support Network: Surround Yourself with Positive...	198
The Importance of a Support Network	198
Strategies for Building a Positive Support Network	200
Examples of Positive Support Networks	203
Overcoming Challenges in Building a Support Network	204
Nurturing Positive Relationships	206
22 Creating a Vision Board: Visualize Success	209
The Power of Visualization	209
Understanding Vision Boards	210
Benefits of Creating a Vision Board	210
Steps to Create an Effective Vision Board	211
Tips for Maximizing the Impact of Your Vision Board	214
Overcoming Common Challenges	215
Practical Exercises for Creating and Using a Vision Board	216
23 Using Positive Self-Talk: Encourage Yourself	218
Understanding Self-Talk The Science Behind	218
Positive Self-Talk Benefits of Positive Self-	219
Talk The Impact of Negative Self-Talk	219
Recognizing Negative Self-Talk Patterns	220
Transforming Negative Self-Talk into	220
Positive Self-Encouragement Techniques for Cultivating Positive Self-Talk Overcoming	221
Challenges in Developing Positive Self-Talk	223

Types of Self-Talk	225
Overcoming Challenges in Positive Self-Talk	227
24 Embracing Failure: Learn from Your Mistakes	229
Redefining Failure The Benefits of Embracing	229
Failure Reframing Failure Strategies for Embracing	230
Failure Learning from Mistakes: A Step-by-Step	231
Approach Examples of Learning from Failure	232
Overcoming the Fear of Failure Practical Exercises	234
to Embrace Failure Practical Exercises to Embrace	235
Failure	236
	237
	239
25 Maintaining Progress: Keep Moving Forward	241
The Importance of Sustained Progress	241
Strategies for Maintaining Progress	242
Overcoming Common Obstacles to Progress	244
Examples of Maintaining Progress in Different Areas	246
Tools and Techniques for Maintaining Progress	247

Introduction

Procrastination is a universal challenge, one that every person faces at some point in their life. Whether it's putting off work tasks, delaying personal projects, or avoiding necessary chores, procrastination can create a cycle of stress, anxiety, and inefficiency. This book is your guide to breaking free from that cycle. It's about understanding why we procrastinate, and more importantly, how to overcome it to lead a more productive, fulfilling life.

What is Procrastination?
Procrastination is the act of delaying or postponing tasks despite knowing there will be negative consequences. It's that nagging feeling of knowing you should be doing something, but choosing to do something else instead. It's the temptation of short-term comfort at the expense of long-term success.

Why We Procrastinate

The reasons behind procrastination are complex and varied. It can stem from fear of failure, perfectionism, lack of motivation, or even the overwhelming nature of the task at hand. Understanding these underlying causes is the first step towards addressing them.

The Cost of Procrastination
Procrastination is not just an innocent habit; it has real consequences. It can lead to missed deadlines, poor performance, stress, and a lower quality of life. On a deeper level, chronic procrastination can erode self-esteem and create a persistent sense of guilt and anxiety.

The Goal of This Book
This book aims to help you understand procrastination, identify your personal triggers, and provide practical strategies to overcome it. Each chapter focuses on a different aspect of productivity and procrastination, offering actionable advice and insights to help you make lasting changes.

Here's a brief overview of the chapters you'll find in this book:

Chapter 1: "Understanding Procrastination: Defining the Enemy"
   In this foundational chapter, we delve into the definition, causes, and effects of procrastination. By understanding the enemy, we can better prepare ourselves to tackle it head-on.

Chapter 2: "Breaking Down Tasks: Divide and Conquer"
   Learn how to break large tasks into smaller, manageable chunks to make them less overwhelming and more achievable.

Chapter 3: "Setting Clear Goals: Aim for Success"
   Discover how to set Specific, Measurable, Achievable, Relevant, and Time-bound (SMART) goals to give your tasks

direction and purpose.

Chapter 4: "Prioritizing Tasks: Focus on What Matters"
Explore the Eisenhower Matrix and other prioritization techniques to focus on what truly matters and avoid getting bogged down by less important tasks.

Chapter 5: "Creating a Schedule: Plan Your Day"
Learn how to create a realistic and effective schedule and stick to it to maximize your productivity.

Chapter 6: "Eliminating Distractions: Minimize Interruptions"
Identify and eliminate common distractions that can derail your focus and productivity.

Chapter 7: "Building Self-Discipline: Develop Good Habits"
Explore strategies to build self-discipline and develop habits that support sustained productivity.

Chapter 8: "Overcoming Fear and Anxiety: Face Your Fears"
Understand how fear and anxiety contribute to procrastination and learn techniques to manage and overcome them.

Chapter 9: "Creating a Conducive Work Environment: Optimize Your Space"
Discover how to create a work environment that supports focus and productivity.

Chapter 10: "Getting Accountability: Find a Study Buddy"
Learn the importance of accountability and how to find

support systems that keep you on track.

Chapter 11: "Rewarding Progress: Celebrate Small Wins"
Explore how to reward yourself for progress and celebrate small wins to stay motivated.

Chapter 12: "Building Resilience: Bounce Back from Failure"
Discover how to build resilience and learn from failures to keep moving forward.

Chapter 13: "Using Technology to Your Advantage: Productivity Tools"
Explore various productivity tools and technologies that can help you stay organized and efficient.

Chapter 14: "Creating a Morning Routine: Start Your Day Right"
Learn how to create a morning routine that sets a positive tone for the rest of the day.

Chapter 15: "Avoiding Multitasking: Focus on One Thing"
Understand the pitfalls of multitasking and learn how to focus on one task at a time for better results.

Chapter 16: "Taking Breaks: Rest and Recharge"
Explore the importance of taking breaks to rest and recharge, and learn how to do so effectively.

Chapter 17: "Seeking Help When Needed: Don't Be Afraid to Ask"
Learn how to seek help when needed and the importance of

not being afraid to ask for support.

Chapter 18: "Staying Motivated: Find Your Why"
Discover how to stay motivated by finding your personal "why" behind your goals.

Chapter 19: "Overcoming Perfectionism: Embrace Imperfection"
Explore how to overcome perfectionism and embrace imperfection to move forward with your tasks.

Chapter 20: "Using Mindfulness: Stay Present and Focused"
Learn how to use mindfulness techniques to stay present and focused on your tasks.

Chapter 21: "Building a Support Network: Surround Yourself with Positive People"
Discover the importance of building a support network and surrounding yourself with positive influences.

Chapter 22: "Creating a Vision Board: Visualize Success"
Explore how to create a vision board to visualize and stay focused on your goals.

Chapter 23: "Using Positive Self-Talk: Encourage Yourself"
Learn how to use positive self-talk to encourage yourself and maintain a positive mindset.

Chapter 24: "Embracing Failure: Learn from Your Mistakes"
Discover how to embrace failure and learn from your mistakes to keep moving forward.

Chapter 25: "Maintaining Progress: Keep Moving Forward"
Explore strategies to maintain progress and keep moving forward even when faced with challenges.

A Personal Journey

Procrastination is deeply personal. What works for one person might not work for another. This book encourages you to experiment with different strategies, find what resonates with you, and tailor your approach to suit your unique circumstances.

Taking the First Step

The first step towards overcoming procrastination is acknowledging it. By picking up this book, you've already taken a significant step in the right direction. This book will serve as your guide, providing you with the tools and insights needed to conquer procrastination and unlock your full potential.

Procrastination is a challenge, but it's not insurmountable. With the right mindset, strategies, and tools, you can overcome it and lead a more productive, fulfilling life. This book is here to help you on that journey, offering practical advice, personal insights, and actionable strategies to tackle procrastination head-on.

Remember, the goal is progress, not perfection. Every small step you take towards overcoming procrastination is a step towards a more productive and fulfilling life. Let's embark on this journey together and make procrastination a thing of the past.

1

Understanding Procrastination: Defining the Enemy

"You may delay, but time will not."
- Benjamin Franklin

Have you ever faced a situation when you had something important to accomplish, but ended up working on something else instead? You never started the task or started but never completed it, even though it was important for you to complete it. We frequently tend to shy away from the most important task at hand and end up scrolling through social media on our phones which is always handy. If you have been through a situation similar to this, when you put off some task at hand, you have already experienced procrastination.

Procrastination is a phenomenon that everyone in this world has experienced knowingly or unknowingly, yet it remains one of the most persistent challenges many people face. Procrastination is a common human behavior that affects people from all walks of life. We all know the feeling of putting off tasks until the last minute, only to be overwhelmed by a looming deadline. But what exactly is procrastination, why do we do it, and what are the consequences, let's dive into it.

> *"Only put off until tomorrow what you are willing to die having left undone."*
> *– Pablo Picasso*

Definition

Procrastination is the act of delaying or postponing tasks intentionally, often to the point of experiencing stress or negative outcomes, which often leads to a habit. It's not just about poor time management, about being lazy or unmotivated; it's a complex behavior influenced by various psychological factors. As author Rita Emmett puts it, "Procrastination is the grave in which opportunity is buried."

Dr. Piers Steel, a leading researcher on procrastination, defines it as "voluntarily putting off an intended course of action despite expecting to be worse off for the delay." This definition highlights a crucial aspect of procrastination – we often know that delaying a task will lead to negative outcomes, yet we do it anyway.

Let us consider Abby, a college student who has a major paper due within a week. Despite her best intentions to start early, she finds herself putting it off day after day every time she has a paper to submit. She knows that waiting until the last minute will result in a lower quality paper and increased stress, yet she can't seem to bring herself to begin. This is procrastination in action.

To better understand procrastination, let's break down its key elements:

1. Delaying Tasks: Choosing to do less important activities instead of more urgent and important ones.
2. Avoiding Tasks: Escaping from tasks that may seem unpleasant or challenging.
3. Inefficiency: Resulting in wasted time, reduced productivity, and increased stress.

> *"Someday is not a day of the week."*
> *– Janet Dailey*

Causes of Procrastination

Let us now understand why we procrastinate. Here are some common causes:

1. Perfectionism: The more important the task, the more important it becomes to make it perfect. The tougher the task, the more expertise it may require to do it. Sometimes it happens that to start on something, some additional knowledge or expertise may be required. While we get busy getting that additional knowledge, the main goal or task often gets delayed and sometimes even forgotten as one task leads to the other like a chain. You may be waiting for the perfect time to start which might never

come.

2. Fear of Failure: Fear of failure is a very common human behavior. Sometimes that fear may lead you to not even start the task instead of making you do it better to avoid failure. Fear often leads to worry and worrying about potential mistakes or negative outcomes can make starting a task seem daunting.

3. Lack of Motivation: If you do not have clearly defined goals or a purpose for doing something, you might not be able to motivate yourself to begin. A goal or purpose always motivates us to do something. Without a clear purpose or interest, it's easy to put off tasks.

4. Overwhelm: Smaller tasks may be easy to accomplish. On the other hand, larger tasks need a lot of our time, energy, and hard work to accomplish. If a task seems daunting, we often end up avoiding it. If that task is something that needs to be done, that too, within a tight deadline, and we delay doing it, it may lead to severe consequences.

5. Distraction: In today's digital age, distractions are everywhere. Social media, emails, and other interruptions can derail our focus. If we keep our phones close to us, we often get distracted by the constant notifications. If we open a message or an email that leads to an article, we often derail from the task at hand and that email or article seems too important to be read immediately.

6. Poor Time Management: Underestimating the time required for a task can lead to procrastination. If you have a pressing task at hand and you don't analyze it properly, you might make a wrong estimation of the time required to finish it. And when you are working on it, it may seem like never-ending. Sometimes a wrong estimation might

even lead to a delayed start.

7. Instant Gratification: Our brains are wired to prefer immediate rewards over future benefits. This makes it challenging to choose long-term goals over short-term pleasures. The bigger the rewards, the tougher the tasks which make people look for shortcuts. Tougher tasks always take more time and patience to complete.

8. Task Aversion: If a task is perceived as unpleasant or difficult, we're more likely to avoid it.

9. Decision Paralysis: When faced with too many choices or a complex task, we might delay action due to feeling overwhelmed. In this kind of situation, people usually pick up the smaller or easier tasks instead of the urgent and important ones.

"A year from now you may wish you had started today."
– Karen Lamb

Effects of Procrastination

Procrastination can have far-reaching effects on various aspects of our lives. Here are some significant impacts:

1. Stress and Anxiety: The worst impact of procrastination is seen when there is a tight deadline approaching. Delaying the start of the task might be pleasing but when the deadline approaches and the work is not done, it leads to a stressful situation. And if there are some challenges

with the task, the stress might be severe. So, it is always better to start early.

2. Reduced Performance: If a delayed start reduces the timeline to accomplish the task, it might lead to a poor quality product or outcome. Rushed work often leads to mistakes, impacting academic, professional, and personal fields.

3. Damaged Reputation: Consistent procrastination can harm your reputation, as others may view you as an unreliable person or a person who lacks commitment.

4. Missed Opportunities: If the right action is not taken at the right time, it may lead to missed opportunities for growth, learning, success, and wealth.

5. Negative Emotional Impact: Chronic procrastination can lead to feelings of guilt, shame, and frustration, creating a negative feedback loop.

6. Health Issues: Chronic procrastination has been linked to various health problems, including insomnia, weakened immune systems, and increased vulnerability to illnesses.

7. Damaged Relationships: Consistently failing to meet commitments can strain personal and professional relationships.

8. Low Self-Esteem: The cycle of procrastination and subsequent feelings of guilt can erode self-confidence over time.

9. Financial Consequences: Putting off important financial decisions or tasks can lead to monetary losses or missed financial opportunities.

"Don't wait for extraordinary circumstance to do good;

try to use ordinary situations."
- Charles Richter

Consider the story of John, a talented graphic designer who consistently procrastinated on client projects. Despite his skills, he found himself losing clients and facing financial difficulties due to missed deadlines and rushed work. The stress of his situation only exacerbated his procrastination, creating a vicious cycle that was hard to break.

Mark, a marketing manager, struggled with procrastination at work. He would delay important projects until the last minute, affecting his team's productivity and his own job satisfaction. Mark's turning point came when he attended a workshop on overcoming procrastination. He learned techniques such as the Pomodoro Technique and task prioritization, which helped him manage his time better and become more efficient at work.

"Think of many things; do one."
- Portuguese proverb

The Psychology Behind Procrastination

Let's dive even deeper into procrastination. To truly understand procrastination, let's understand the underlying psychological mechanisms at play. One key concept is "time inconsistency" – the tendency for people to value immediate rewards more highly than future rewards. Our brains are wired to prioritize short-term benefits over long-term gains. This is why it's so easy to choose watching TV now over working on a project that will benefit us in the future.

Another important psychological factor is the concept of "present bias." This refers to the tendency to give stronger weight to payoffs that are closer to the present time when considering trade-offs between two future moments. It explains why we often make plans to start a diet "next week" or begin a new exercise routine "on Monday," but when the time comes, we push it off again.

Procrastination makes easy things hard, hard things harder.
- Mason Cooley

As psychologist Daniel Kahneman explains in his book "Thinking, Fast and Slow," our minds operate in two systems: System 1, which is fast, instinctive, and emotional; and System 2, which is slower, more deliberative, and more logical. Procrastination often occurs when our emotional System 1 overrides the logical planning of System 2.

While procrastination can feel like an insurmountable obstacle, it's important to remember that it's a habit that can be overcome. As motivational speaker Denis Waitley once said, "Procrastination is the fear of success. People procrastinate because they are afraid of the success that they know will result if they move ahead now. Because success is heavy and carries a responsibility with it, it is much easier to procrastinate and live on the 'someday I'll' philosophy."

> *"Know the true value of time; snatch, seize, and enjoy every moment of it. No idleness, no laziness, no procrastination: never put off till tomorrow what you can do today."*
> *– Philip Stanhope, 4th Earl of Chesterfield*

Recognizing procrastination as a form of self-sabotage is the first step toward overcoming it. By understanding the underlying causes and effects of procrastination, we can develop strategies to combat it effectively. Procrastination is a complex enemy that affects virtually everyone at some point in their lives. By defining it, understanding its causes, and recognizing its effects, we take the first crucial step in overcoming this pervasive habit.

As we move forward in this book, we'll explore various strategies and techniques to combat procrastination effectively. We'll learn how to harness our motivation, manage our time more efficiently, and develop the mental resilience needed to tackle tasks head-on.

Let's end this chapter with a humorous quote.

> *Procrastination is like a credit card: it's a lot of fun until you get the bill.*
> *– Christopher Parker*

2

Breaking Down Tasks: Divide and Conquer

"Nothing is particularly hard if you divide it into small jobs."
– Henry Ford

We learned in the first chapter that one of the causes of procrastination is overwhelming. If a task seems too big, we tend to procrastinate. We try to avoid doing it or delay as long as possible. One of the most effective strategies to combat procrastination is to break down larger tasks into smaller, more manageable tasks. This approach, often referred to as "divide and conquer," can make daunting projects feel less overwhelming and more achievable. In this chapter, we'll explore the benefits of breaking down tasks, practical methods on how to do it, and real-life examples to illustrate the process.

"The secret of getting ahead is getting started. The

secret of getting started is breaking your complex overwhelming tasks into small manageable tasks, and then starting on the first one."
– Mark Twain

The Art of Breaking Down Tasks

Breaking down tasks is a powerful strategy in the battle against procrastination. It's the process of dividing large, complex projects into smaller, more manageable parts. This approach not only makes the task less daunting but also provides a clear roadmap for completion.

As the ancient Chinese philosopher Lao Tzu wisely said, "The journey of a thousand miles begins with a single step." This proverb perfectly encapsulates the philosophy behind task breakdown. By focusing on the individual steps rather than the entire journey, we can overcome that hurdle that often accompanies large tasks.

Why Breaking Down Tasks Works

1. Reduces Overwhelm: Large tasks can trigger anxiety and a sense of being overwhelmed. Breaking them down makes them feel more approachable.
2. Provides Clear Starting Points: With smaller tasks, it's easier to identify where to begin, reducing the likelihood of procrastination.
3. OffersaSenseofProgress: Completingsubtasksprovides regular doses of accomplishment, boosting motivation

and momentum.
4. Improves Focus: Smaller tasks are easier to concentrate on, leading to improved productivity and quality of work.
5. Enhances Time Management: Breaking down tasks allows for more accurate time estimation and scheduling.

> *"Small deeds done are better than great deeds planned."*
> *– Peter Marshall*

Practical Methods for Breaking Down Tasks

Here are some practical methods to help you divide and conquer:

1. Task Lists: Create a detailed task list by breaking the project into smaller, actionable steps. For example, if you need to write a research paper, your list might include: choosing a topic, conducting research, creating an outline, writing the introduction, drafting body paragraphs, and editing.

2. The Pomodoro Technique: This time management method involves working in short, focused intervals (typically 25 minutes) followed by a short break. Breaking your work into these intervals can make large tasks more manageable and improve focus.

3. Milestones: Set milestones for your project. For example, if you're working on a month-long project, identify key goals to achieve each week. This provides a roadmap and helps track progress.

4. Chunking: Group related tasks together. For instance, if

you're planning a presentation, you might chunk tasks into research, slide creation, and rehearsal.

5. Reverse Engineering: Start with the end goal and work backward to identify all the steps needed to reach that goal. This method helps ensure that no crucial steps are overlooked.

Let's look at how this might work in practice. Kate, a postgrad- uate student, has been procrastinating on writing her master's thesis. The task seems overwhelming, so she decides to break it down:

End Goal: Complete a 300-page thesis on a subject for her post-graduation.

Major Components:

- Literaturereview
- Methodology
- Datacollection
- Dataanalysis
- Results
- Discussion
- Conclusion

Break Down Components:

- Identifykeyareasofresearch
- Findandreadrelevantpapers
- Summarizefindings
- Writeareviewdraft

Create Subtasks: Find and read relevant papers:

- Searchacademicdatabasesforpapersonthetopic
- Download20mostrelevantpapers
- Readandtakenoteson5papersperweek
- Createannotatedbibliography

By breaking down her thesis into manageable chunks, Kate can focus on one small task at a time, making steady progress without feeling overwhelmed.

Overcoming Common Challenges

While breaking down tasks is a powerful strategy, it's not without its challenges. Here are some common issues that you might face while doing divide and conquer.

1. Over-complicating the breakdown: While breaking down the tasks, you should be mindful that the tasks should not be big and tough. Your goal is to break down the bigger task into small, easy tasks. Break tasks down enough to make them manageable, but not so much that the breakdown itself becomes overwhelming.

2. Losing focus on your end goal: You should not break down tasks in such a way that your entire time and energy go into finishing the smaller tasks and while doing so, you forget what you were trying to achieve. You should regularly review your end goal and how each subtask contributes to it.

3. Underestimating time for small tasks: If you make a wrong estimation of the time needed to finish each and

every smaller task, then you might need more time to finish the overall tasks. If smaller tasks take more time, it might again lead to procrastination as each task would seem overwhelming.

4. Procrastinating Divide and Conquer: Remember that breaking down the bigger tasks into smaller ones doesn't automatically cure procrastination. You might find yourself putting off even the smaller tasks.

> *"The man who moves a mountain begins by carrying away small stones."*
> *– Confucius*

Tools for Task Breakdown

Several tools can assist in breaking down and managing tasks:

1. Mind Mapping Software: Tools like MindMeister or Microsoft Whiteboard help visualize the breakdown of complex projects.
2. Project Management Apps: Trello, Asana, or Microsoft To-Do allow you to create task lists, set deadlines, and track progress.
3. BulletJournaling: Thisanalogsystemcanbeaneffective way to break down and track tasks on paper.
4. Spreadsheets: Simple yet powerful, spreadsheets like Google Sheets or Excel can be used to create detailed task breakdowns.

Remember, the best tool is the one you'll use consistently and that works for you.

Let's look at some real-life examples to illustrate how breaking down tasks can be effective. Jane, a freelance writer, faced the daunting task of writing a 50,000-word novel. The sheer length of the project paralyzed her. To overcome this, she broke the novel down into chapters, and each chapter into scenes. She set a daily word count goal of 1,000 words, focusing on one scene at a time. By doing this, Jane was able to complete her novel within three months.

Bill, a project manager, was responsible for launching a new product. Theprojectinvolvedmultipleteamsandatight deadline. Bill broke the project down into phases: research, development, marketing, and launch. Each phase was further divided into specific tasks, with deadlines assigned to each team member. By managing the project in smaller steps, Bill ensured that the team stayed on track and the product was launched successfully.

Techniques to Implement Immediately

To put the divide and conquer strategy into action, here are some techniques you can start using right away:

1. Daily To-Do Lists: Write a to-do list the night before, breaking down your day's work into smaller tasks. Prioritize the most important tasks and tackle them first.
2. Set Time Limits: Allocate specific time slots for each task. This prevents you from spending too much time on one task and neglecting others.
3. Use Tools and Apps: Utilize productivity apps like Trello, Asana, or Todoist to organize and track your tasks. These

tools can help you break down tasks and monitor your progress.
4. Reward Yourself: Give yourself small rewards after completing tasks. This can provide motivation and make the process more enjoyable.

We have reached the end of this chapter and I would like to tell you that divide and conquer is just a mindset shift. Instead of seeing a large task as one task, you should develop the mindset of seeing it as a collection of smaller ones. If you develop this habit, no task will seem overwhelming to you.

No bigger task will seem to you like an insurmountable obstacle but as a series of achievable steps. By breaking them down, you make the impossible possible, one step at a time. As author Robert Collier once said, "Success is the sum of small efforts, repeated day in and day out."

By mastering the art of task breakdown, you're not just combating procrastination – you're setting yourself up for success in all areas of life. Whether you're writing a thesis, launching a business, or simply trying to declutter your home, the principle remains the same: divide and conquer.

By breaking down tasks into smaller ones, you reduce overwhelm, increase your focus, and build momentum. So the next time you find yourself staring at your personal Mount Everest, take a deep breath, break it down, and take that first small step. Before you know it, you'll be standing at the summit, marveling at how far you've come.

As you apply these techniques, you'll find that large tasks become less intimidating and more achievable. Remember, the journey of a thousand miles begins with a single step. By breaking down your tasks and taking them one step at a time, you can conquer procrastination and achieve your goals. Are you ready to divide and conquer?

3

Setting Clear Goals: Aim for Success

"A goal is a dream with a deadline"
- Napoleon Hill

Everybody wants to achieve something in life. Everybody has dreams. You, too will have dreams. Now, if you just add a deadline to a dream, it becomes a goal. It is that simple. Goals give a purpose and a direction to your life.

Setting clear goals is a cornerstone of productivity and a powerful antidote to procrastination. When you know exactly what you want to achieve, it's easier to focus your efforts and stay motivated.

Imagine you're an archer. You have your bow in hand, arrow nocked, ready to shoot. But there's one problem: you can't see the target. How likely are you to hit it? This scenario illustrates the importance of clear, well-defined goals in overcoming procrastination and achieving success.

The Power of Goal Setting

Goal setting is more than just deciding what you want to accomplish. It's about creating a clear, actionable plan that guides your efforts and motivates you to overcome procrastination. As the famous management consultant Peter Drucker once said, "What gets measured, gets managed." This principle is at the

heart of effective goal setting.

> *"Setting goals is the first step in turning the invisible into the visible."*
> *– Tony Robbins*

The Importance of Goal Setting

Goals provide direction and purpose. Without clear goals, it's easy to drift aimlessly, losing focus and motivation. Here are some key reasons why goal setting is crucial:

1. Clarity: Goals help clarify what you want to achieve, making it easier to plan and take action. Only if you know what you want, you can have it.
2. Motivation: Goals motivate you to keep going. When you have a plan and work on it and you can move forward, and achieve step by step as per the plan, you are motivated to keep going.
3. Focus: Goals help focus your time and energy effectively. Your productivity increases when you are focused on what you want to achieve without distraction.
4. Measurement: Goals offer you a way of measuring progress and success. Anything that can be measured can

be achieved.

5. Accountability: Setting goals makes you accountable to yourself and others, fostering commitment and discipline. Goals don't let you derail from your path.

6. Overcoming Procrastination: Specific goals make tasks feel more concrete and actionable, reducing the tendency to procrastinate.

SMART Goals

In 1981, George T. Doran introduced the concept of SMART goals in his paper "There's a S.M.A.R.T. Way to Write Management's Goals and Objectives." SMART is an acronym that stands for Specific, Measurable, Achievable, Relevant, and Time-bound. This framework has since become a cornerstone in goal-setting practices across various fields, helping individuals and organizations set clear and attainable objectives.

Understanding SMART Goals

Let's break down each component:

1. Specific: A goal should be very very specific. It should be clearly defined so that it sets into our brains. Only if it is defined clearly, our subconscious mind can work on it. For example, instead of saying "I want to get fit," a specific goal would be "I lose 10 pounds in 3 months by exercising 4 times a week and following a healthy diet."

2. Measurable: A measurable goal means quantifying your goal. When you define a goal, it should be measured by a unit of measurement available in mathematics. For

example, "I save $5,000 in one year" is measurable because you can track your savings over time. The goal "I run 5 miles every morning" is measurable while "I run every day is not".

3. Achievable: An achievable goal is realistic and attainable, considering your current resources and constraints. It should challenge you but still be possible. It's true that you should set your mind to achieve anything in life, but you should also be aware of your own capabilities. For instance, "I want to run a marathon in six months" is achievable if you are already running regularly and can commit to a training schedule.

4. Relevant: A relevant goal aligns with your broader objectives and values. It answers the question, "Why is this goal important to me?" For example, "I want to improve my public speaking skills to advance my career" is relevant if career advancement is a priority for you. You should not set a goal because your friend achieved something. If your neighbor buys an expensive car, you should not set the same goal if you do not need an expensive car or if your current financial priorities are something else.

5. Time-bound: A goal always has a deadline. A goal without a deadline is just a wish. For instance, "I am XYZ certified by 5 pm, December 31st, 2024" sets a clear timeframe for completion whereas "I am XYZ certified" is not.

Crafting Your SMART Goals

To create your own SMART goals, follow these steps:

1. Define Your Objective: Start with a broad objective. What do you want to achieve? This could be related to your career, health, personal growth, or any other area of life.
2. Make It Specific: Narrow down your objective to a specific goal. Who is involved? What exactly do you want to accomplish? Where and when will it happen? Why is it important?
3. Ensure it's Measurable: Determine how you will measure progress. What metrics or indicators will you use? How will you know when you've achieved your goal?
4. Check for Feasibility: Assess whether your goal is realistic. Do you have the necessary resources, skills, and time? Is it within your control?
5. Confirm its Relevance: Reflect on the significance of your goal. Does it align with your long-term objectives? Is it worthwhile and meaningful?
6. Set a Deadline: Give a deadline for your goal. When do you want to achieve your goal? Setting milestones along the way can help track progress.

You can read my book Goals Mastery Manual to learn more about Goal Setting. It is available on Amazon. In this book, I have defined a 7 step framework to achieve goals.

1. Determine your goals: First, determine what you want to achieve. List your dreams as if everything will be fulfilled.
2. Find key areas: Divide your goals into key areas of your

life such as career, finance, health, and relationships.
3. Most important goal: Select the most important goals under each area to focus only on the life-changing goals.
4. Analyze your goals: Analyze the goals picked to make them more real so that they transform from dreams.
5. Acquire additional skills: Decide if any additional skills are required before working on the goals and acquiring them.
6. Decide deadlines: Decide the deadline for each and every goal so that you feel driven and motivated.
7. Make an action plan: Make an action plan for your goals about how you are going to achieve them.

"You are never too old to set another goal or to dream a new dream."
– C.S. Lewis

Let's consider some examples related to real-time scenarios that will help you better understand goal setting. Mark is working in sales and marketing, is unhappy in his current job, and wants to change careers. He learned about web development from his friend. Recently he saw an advertisement for a 12-month coding bootcamp that can help him transition to a web developer and work as a developer in software companies. Here's how he might use SMART goals:

Initial Objective: "I want to change careers."

Considering today is 26 July 2024 and the coding boot camp starts on 1 August, considering an additional month to switch jobs after the course is completed, Mark's goal should look like this. He can have 2 goals.

"I complete a coding boot camp on web development by 5 pm, 31 July 2025 and build a portfolio of up to five projects and I apply 2 jobs per week in the last 2 months."

"I work as a web developer in a software company by 5 pm, 31 August 2025."

How is this goal SMART?

- Specific: Clearlydefinesthecareerchangefrommarketing to web development
- Measurable: Includes concrete deliverables (boot camp completion, five projects, job application numbers).
- Achievable: Allows a realistic timeframe for learning and job searching.
- Relevant: Aligns with Mark's desire for a career change.
- Time-bound: A 12-month deadline.

Overcoming Common Goal-Setting Pitfalls

Even with the SMART framework, goal setting can have its challenges. Here are some common pitfalls and how to avoid them:

Setting Too Many Goals
 Having too many goals can lead to overwhelm and, ironically, procrastination.
 Solution: Prioritize your goals. Focus on one or two key

objectives at a time.

Setting Unrealistic Goals

While ambition is good, setting impossible goals can be demotivating.

Solution: Be honest about your current abilities and circumstances. It's okay to dream big but break those big dreams into achievable milestones.

Neglecting to Review and Adjust

Goals aren't set in stone. Circumstances change, and your goals may need to change too.

Solution: Schedule regular goal review sessions. Be willing to adjust your goals as needed.

Focusing Solely on the Outcome

While the end result is important, focusing only on the outcome can be overwhelming.

Solution: Break your goal into smaller process goals. Celebrate progress along the way.

Forgetting to Reward Yourself

Achieving goals takes hard work. If you don't acknowledge your successes, you may lose motivation.

Solution: Build rewards into your goal-setting process. Celebrate both small wins and major achievements.

> *"By recording your dreams and goals on paper, you set in motion the process of becoming the person you most want to be."*
> *– Mark Victor Hansen*

The goal-setting process itself is a powerful antidote to procrastination. By taking the time to clearly define what you want to achieve, you're already taking action towards your dreams. As you move forward, keep in mind the words of motivational speaker Zig Ziglar: "A goal properly set is halfway reached." With the help of goal setting, you're not just aiming for success – you're actively moving towards it.

Setting clear, SMART goals is a powerful strategy for overcoming procrastination and achieving success. By making your goals Specific, Measurable, Achievable, Relevant, and Time-bound, you create a roadmap for action and progress. As you apply these principles, you'll find that your goals become more attainable, and your path to success becomes clearer. Choose an area of your life where you've been procrastinating, and try setting a SMART goal. You might be surprised at how quickly you start making progress once your target is clear.

4

Prioritizing Tasks: Focus on What Matters

"Your life is a reflection of your priorities."
– Unknown

Prioritization is the process of determining the order and importance of tasks based on their urgency and significance. It's about making conscious choices about where to focus your time and energy. Without a clear sense of priority, it's easy to get overwhelmed and distracted by less important tasks.

In our fast-paced world, where the demands on our time and attention are constantly increasing, effective prioritization is essential. Learning to prioritize effectively is a crucial skill in overcoming procrastination and achieving your goals. As the famous author Stephen Covey once said, "The key is not to prioritize what's on your schedule, but to schedule your priorities."

One of the most powerful tools for prioritizing tasks is the Eisenhower Matrix. In this chapter, we'll explore how to use the Eisenhower Matrix to focus on what truly matters and achieve greater productivity.

The Importance of Prioritizing Tasks

Prioritizing tasks helps you to:

1. Enhance Productivity: By focusing on high-priority tasks, you can achieve more in less time.
2. Reduce Stress: Clear priorities help prevent the overwhelm that comes from juggling too many tasks.
3. Improve Decision-Making: Prioritization provides a framework for making decisions about how to spend your time and resources.
4. Achieve Goals: By prioritizing tasks that align with your goals, you move closer to achieving them.
5. Maintain Balance: Effective prioritization helps you balance different aspects of your life, ensuring that important areas receive the attention they deserve.

The Eisenhower Matrix: A Tool for Effective Prioritization

The Eisenhower Matrix, named after former U.S. President Dwight D. Eisenhower, is a powerful tool for prioritizing tasks based on their urgency and importance. Eisenhower, known for his efficient time management skills, developed this matrix to help make decisions about which tasks to tackle first.

The Eisenhower Matrix divides tasks into four quadrants based on two criteria: urgency and importance. Here's how it works:

The matrix is divided into four quadrants:

- Quadrant I: Urgent and Important – Tasks that need immediate attention.
- Quadrant II: Not Urgent but Important – Tasks that are important for long-term goals and should be scheduled.
- Quadrant III: Urgent but Not Important – Tasks that should be delegated if possible.
- Quadrant IV: Not Urgent and Not Important – Tasks that are distractions and can be eliminated.

By categorizing tasks into these quadrants, you can focus on what truly matters and avoid getting overwhelmed by less important activities.

> *"Things which matter most must never be at the mercy of things which matter least."*
> *– Johann Wolfgang von Goethe*

Let's break down each quadrant in detail:

Quadrant I: Urgent and Important (Do First)

Tasks in this quadrant require immediate attention and are crucial to achieving your goals. They often involve deadlines or crises that cannot be ignored. Examples include:

- Meetingprojectdeadlines
- Handlingurgentworkcrises
- Addressinghealthemergencies

Example: Jane has an urgent report due by the end of the day for a crucial client meeting tomorrow. This task is both urgent and important, so it belongs in Quadrant I and should be done first.

Quadrant II: Not Urgent but Important (Schedule)

Tasks in this quadrant are important for long-term success but do not require immediate attention. They often involve planning, development, and personal growth. Examples include:

- Strategicplanning
- Professionaldevelopment
- Buildingrelationships
- Healthandexercise

Example: John wants to improve his public speaking skills to advance his career. Although this task is important, it is not urgent, so it belongs in Quadrant II. John should schedule regular practice sessions.

Quadrant III: Urgent but Not Important (Delegate)

Tasks in this quadrant demand immediate attention but are not critical to achieving your goals. They can often be delegated to others. Examples include:

- Interruptionsfromcolleagues
- Routinemeetings
- Minorrequests

Example: Sarah receives frequent requests from her team for minor technical support. These tasks are urgent but not critical to her primary role. Sarah can delegate these tasks to the IT support team.

Quadrant IV: Not Urgent and Not Important (Eliminate)

Tasks in this quadrant are neither urgent nor important and do not contribute to your goals. They are often time-wasters and should be minimized or eliminated. Examples include:

- Excessivesocialmediabrowsing
- WatchingTVshowswithoutpurpose
- Unproductiveactivities

Example: Mark spends a significant amount of time scrolling through social media during work hours. This task is neither urgent nor important, so it belongs in Quadrant IV and should be eliminated or minimized.

Using the Eisenhower Matrix

1. List Your Tasks

Start by listing all the tasks you need to accomplish. Don't worry about prioritizing them yet; just get them all down.

2. Assess Each Task

For each task, ask yourself two questions:

- Is this task urgent? (Does it need to be done soon?)

- Is this task important? (Does it contribute significantly to my goals or values?)

3. Place Tasks in the Appropriate Quadrant

Based on your assessment, place each task in the corresponding quadrant of the matrix.

4. Take Action

Now that your tasks are organized, take action based on their quadrant:

- Quadrant 1: Do these tasks right away

- Quadrant 2: Schedule time for these tasks

- Quadrant 3: Delegate if possible, or do after Quadrant 1 tasks

- Quadrant 4: Eliminate these tasks

Let's see how this might work in practice. Jill, a marketing manager, has the following tasks on her plate:

- Prepare for tomorrow's client presentation (Urgent and Important - Quadrant 1)

- Respond to emails (Urgent but Not Important - Quadrant 3)

- Work on long-term marketing strategy (Important but Not Urgent - Quadrant 2)

- Organize desk drawer (Neither Urgent nor Important - Quadrant 4)

- Call team meeting to discuss project delays (Urgent and Important - Quadrant 1)
- Browse social media (Neither Urgent nor Important - Quadrant 4)
- Complete monthly report due next week (Important but Not Urgent - Quadrant 2)
- Return client's call from this morning (Urgent and Important - Quadrant 1)

Using the Eisenhower Matrix, Jill can prioritize her day:

1. She'll focus first on preparing for the client presentation, calling the team meeting, and returning the client's call.
2. She'll schedule time later in the week to work on the long-term strategy and monthly report.
3. She'll set aside a specific time to batch-process emails, rather than responding to each one as it comes in.
4. She'll eliminate browsing social media and organizing her desk drawer, recognizing these as low-value activities.

Overcoming Common Prioritization Challenges

Even with a tool like the Eisenhower Matrix, prioritization can be challenging. Here are some common issues and how to address them:

Everything Seems Urgent and Important
When everything feels like a Quadrant 1 task, it's easy to become overwhelmed.
Solution: Be more critical in your assessment. Ask yourself, "What would happen if I didn't do this task?" This can help

you distinguish between truly urgent and important tasks and those that just feel that way.

Difficulty Delegating

Some people struggle to delegate Quadrant 3 tasks, feeling they need to do everything themselves.
Solution: Remember that delegating frees you up for more important tasks. Start small, delegating one or two tasks, and gradually increase as you become more comfortable.

Neglecting Quadrant 2

It's easy to get caught up in urgent tasks and neglect the important but not urgent Quadrant 2 activities.
Solution: Schedule a specific time for Quadrant 2 tasks. Treat this time as you would any other important appointment.

Overestimating Available Time

We often underestimate how long tasks will take, leading to over-commitment.
Solution: Use the "Planning Fallacy" principle we discussed earlier. Estimate how long you think a task will take, then double it for a more realistic timeframe.

Failing to Re-evaluate Regularly

Priorities can shift quickly. What's important today might not be tomorrow.
Solution: Make it a habit to review and adjust your priorities regularly. A daily review can be helpful.

> *"You have to decide what your highest priorities are*
> *and have the courage – pleasantly, smilingly,*

non-apologetically – to say 'no' to other things. And the way to do that is by having a bigger 'yes' burning inside."
– Stephen R. Covey

Techniques to Maintain Focus on Priorities

To maintain focus on your priorities, consider these techniques:

1. DailyReview: Starteachdaybyreviewingyourtasksand categorizing them using the Eisenhower Matrix.
2. Set Clear Goals: Ensure that your tasks align with your long-term goals and values.
3. Time Blocking: Allocate specific blocks of time for tasks in Quadrants I and II.
4. Limit Distractions: Minimize interruptions and distractions, especially for tasks in Quadrants I and II.
5. Regular Reflection: Periodically review your priorities and adjust as needed to stay aligned with your goals.

Prioritization is more than a time management technique—it's a way of ensuring that your actions align with your values and goals. By using tools like the Eisenhower Matrix, you're not just managing your time more effectively—you're making conscious choices about how to invest your energy and focus. This clarity can be a powerful antidote to procrastination, as it becomes easier to tackle tasks when you understand their true importance.

Remember, the key to success lies in focusing on high-priority tasks and minimizing or delegating lower-priority ones. Are you ready to prioritize your tasks and achieve greater success?

5

Creating a Schedule: Plan Your Day

"Lost time is never found again."
– Benjamin Franklin

Creating and sticking to a schedule is a crucial step in managing your time effectively and overcoming procrastination. A well-structured schedule helps you allocate your time wisely, ensures that important tasks are completed, and provides a sense of control over your day. In this chapter, we'll explore practical strategies for creating a schedule that works for you and tips for maintaining it consistently.

Imagine trying to navigate a complex maze without a map. You might eventually find your way out, but you'd waste a lot of time and energy in the process. Similarly, approaching your day without a well-planned schedule is like trying to navigate that maze blindfolded. A good schedule acts as your daily roadmap, guiding you efficiently through your tasks and helping you overcome the hurdle of procrastination.

Scheduling is more than just jotting down a to-do list. It's about strategically allocating your time and energy to maximize productivity and minimize stress. As the famous saying goes, "Failing to plan is planning to fail." This couldn't be more true when it comes to managing your time effectively.

The Benefits of a Structured Schedule

A structured schedule offers numerous benefits:

1. Increased Productivity: A schedule helps you focus on tasks that need to be done, reducing time wasted on unimportant activities.
2. Reduced Stress: Knowing what needs to be done and when it needs to be done reduces anxiety and stress.
3. Better Time Management: A schedule allows you to allocate time appropriately for different tasks, ensuring that nothing is overlooked.
4. Improved Work-Life Balance: By scheduling both work and personal activities, you can maintain a healthier balance between different areas of your life.
5. Enhanced Accountability: A schedule helps you stay accountable to yourself and others, fostering discipline and consistency.
6. Procrastination Prevention: A clear schedule leaves less room for procrastination.

> "Time is what we want most, but what we use worst."
> – William Penn

Creating an Effective Schedule

Creating a schedule that works for you is part science, part art. Here's a step-by-step guide to crafting a schedule that will boost your productivity and help you stick to your plans:

Identify Your Priorities

Start by identifying your most important tasks and goals. What needs to be accomplished? Prioritize tasks based on urgency and importance, using tools like the Eisenhower Matrix discussed in the previous chapter.

Identify Your Peak Productivity Hours

We all have times of day when we're naturally more focused and energetic. Identify your "golden hours" and schedule your most important or challenging tasks during these times.

Use Time Blocking

Time blocking involves dedicating specific blocks of time to certain tasks or types of work. For example, you might block out 9-11 AM for focused work on a major project, 11 AM-12 PM for responding to emails, etc.

Include Buffer Time

Don't schedule every minute of your day. Leave buffer time between tasks for unexpected interruptions or overruns. A good rule of thumb is to leave about 20% of your day unscheduled.

Be Realistic: Ensure that your schedule is realistic and achievable. Avoid overloading your day with too many tasks, which can lead to burnout and frustration.

Schedule Breaks

Regular breaks are crucial for maintaining focus and preventing burnout. Include short breaks every 60-90 minutes, and longer breaks for meals.

Plan for Self-Care

Don't forget to schedule time for exercise, relaxation, and activities you enjoy. These are crucial for maintaining overall well-being and productivity.

Use the Right Tools

Choose a scheduling tool that works for you. This could be a digital calendar, a paper planner, or a specialized app. The best tool is the one you'll actually use consistently.

Review and Adjust Regularly

At the end of each day or week, review your schedule. What worked? What didn't? Adjust your future schedules based on these insights.

Let's see how effective scheduling might look in practice. Mark, a freelance graphic designer, used to struggle with procrastination and missed deadlines. Here's how he restructured his day using effective scheduling techniques:

- 6:00AM-7:00AM:MorningRoutine(Exercise,Meditation, Breakfast)
- 7:00AM-8:00AM:PlanandPrioritize(Reviewtasks,set goals for the day)

- 8:00 AM - 10:00 AM: Deep Work Session (Focus on high-priority tasks)
- 10:00 AM - 10:15 AM: Break
- 10:15 AM - 12:00 PM: Continued Work (Complete remaining tasks)
- 12:00 PM - 1:00 PM: Lunch Break
- 1:00 PM - 3:00 PM: Meetings/Collaborative Work
- 3:00 PM - 3:15 PM: Break
- 3:15 PM - 5:00 PM: Admin Tasks/Email Management
- 5:00 PM - 6:00 PM: Wrap-Up and Plan for Tomorrow
- 6:00 PM - 7:00 PM: Dinner and Relaxation
- 7:00 PM - 9:00 PM: Personal Time (Hobbies, Family, Leisure)
- 9:00 PM - 10:00 PM: Wind Down (Reading, Reflection)
- 10:00 PM: Bedtime

Notice how Mark has:

- Scheduled his most challenging work during his peak productivity hours in the morning
- Included regular breaks
- Used time blocking for focused work
- Left some buffer time in case tasks run over
- Planned for self-care (exercise, breaks, free time in the evening)

You can maintain a daily planner like this available on Amazon.

Overcoming Common Scheduling Challenges

Even with the best intentions, sticking to a schedule can be challenging. Here are some common issues and how to address them:

Over-scheduling

It's tempting to pack your schedule full, but this often leads to stress and burnout.

Solution: Be realistic about what you can accomplish in a day. Remember to include buffer time and breaks.

Unexpected Interruptions

Life doesn't always go according to plan, and unexpected tasks or emergencies can throw off your schedule.

Solution: Build flexibility into your schedule. The buffer time we mentioned earlier can be crucial here.

Lack of Motivation

Sometimes, even with a clear schedule, you might struggle to get started on tasks.

Solution: Commit to working on a task for just 20 minutes. Often, getting started is the hardest part, and you'll find yourself continuing beyond the 20 minutes.

Procrastination on Unpleasant Tasks

We tend to put off tasks we don't enjoy, even when they're on our schedule.

Solution: Schedule your most unpleasant or challenging task first thing in the day. Everything after that will feel easier in comparison. You can also use the Eisenhower Matrix in this regard.

Difficulty Saying No

Taking on too many commitments can overcrowd your schedule.

Solution: Practice saying no to non-essential requests. Remember, every time you say "yes" to someone, you say "no" to yourself.

> *"The key is in not spending time, but in investing it."*
> *– Stephen R. Covey*

Let us discuss some more real-life scenarios that will help you understand scheduling.

Lisa, a marketing manager, struggled to balance her numerous responsibilities. She started by listing all her tasks and categorizing them using the Eisenhower Matrix. She then created a daily schedule, allocating specific time blocks for meetings, deep work, and administrative tasks. By sticking to her schedule and adjusting it as needed, Lisa was able to manage her workload more effectively and reduce stress.

James, a college student, found it challenging to keep up with his studies and extracurricular activities. He created a weekly schedule, dedicating time blocks for classes, study sessions, part-time work, and social activities. James also included buffer time for unexpected assignments and personal relaxation. This structured approach helped him stay on top of his responsibilities and maintain a healthy work-life balance.

Creating and sticking to a schedule is a powerful tool in the fight against procrastination. As motivational speaker Jim Rohn once said, "Either you run the day, or the day runs you." With an effective schedule, you're putting yourself firmly in the driver's seat of your day.

Remember, the goal of scheduling isn't to turn you into a robot, rigidly following a predetermined plan. Instead, it's about creating a structure that supports your goals, maximizes your productivity, and reduces the mental load of constant decision-making.

As you move forward, experiment with different scheduling techniques to find what works best for you. Be patient with yourself – developing new habits takes time. Celebrate the small wins as you become more adept at planning and following through on your daily schedule.

Are you ready to create a schedule that works for you and start planning your day for success?

> "You may delay, but time will not."
> – Benjamin Franklin

6

Eliminating Distractions: Minimize Interruptions

"Starve your distractions, feed your focus."
– Unknown

In our hyper-connected world, distractions are everywhere, from buzzing notifications to constant interruptions. These distractions can significantly hinder productivity and make it difficult to stay focused on tasks. To overcome procrastination and achieve your goals, it's crucial to identify and eliminate distractions. In this chapter, we'll explore strategies for recognizing common distractions and implementing effective techniques to minimize interruptions.

The Cost of Distractions

Distractions are more than just minor annoyances. They have a real, measurable impact on our productivity and well-being. Studies have shown that it can take up to 23 minutes to fully regain focus after an interruption. In a workday filled with constant distractions, this lost time adds up quickly.

As the famous psychologist and author Daniel Goleman notes, "Attention is a limited resource, like money. You can spend it on many things, but when it's gone, it's gone."

Understanding the Impact of Distractions

Distractions can derail your productivity in several ways:

1. Reduced Focus: Frequent interruptions break your concentration, making it harder to stay engaged with tasks.
2. Increased Stress: Juggling multiple distractions can lead to stress and a feeling of being overwhelmed.
3. Lower Quality of Work: Constant distractions can lead to mistakes and lower the overall quality of your work.
4. Decreased Efficiency: Switching between tasks due to interruptions can waste time and decrease efficiency.
5. Procrastination: Distractions often serve as a way to procrastinate, delaying important tasks.

> *"The successful warrior is the average man, with laser-like focus."*
> *– Bruce Lee*

Identifying Common Distractions

To effectively eliminate distractions, it's important to first identify them. Common distractions include:

1. Digital Distractions: Social media, email notifications, text messages, and online browsing.
2. Environmental Distractions: Noise, clutter, and interruptions from colleagues or family members.
3. Internal Distractions: Thoughts, worries, and mental fatigue.
4. Task Switching: Frequently switching between tasks without completing them.

To identify your specific distractions, try this exercise:

For one week, keep a "distraction log." Every time you find yourself distracted, jot down:
 - What distracted you
 - What you were working on when you got distracted
 - How long the distraction lasted
 - How you felt after the distraction

This log will help you identify patterns and your most common distractions.

Let's see how these strategies might work in practice. Mark, a software developer, has been struggling with distractions. Here's how he implements distraction-elimination strategies:

7:30 AM: Mark starts his day with a 10-minute meditation session to center his mind.

8:00 AM: He reviews his to-do list and schedules his day, including specific "focus blocks" for deep work.

9:00 AM: Before starting work, Mark puts his phone on "Do Not Disturb" mode and places it out of sight.

9:05 AM: He uses a website blocker to restrict access to social media sites during work hours.

9:10 AM: Mark puts on noise-cancelling headphones and starts his first Pomodoro session.

12:00 PM: During lunch, he takes a walk outside, giving his mind a complete break from work.

1:00 PM: For his afternoon focus block, Mark hangs a "Deep Work in Progress" sign on his office door.

5:00 PM: At the end of the day, Mark reviews his progress and plans for tomorrow, helping to clear his mind for the evening.

By implementing these strategies, Mark significantly reduces distractions and improves his focus and productivity.

Overcoming Common Eliminating Distraction Challenges

Even with the best strategies, eliminating distractions can be challenging. Here are some common issues and how to address them:

FOMO (Fear of Missing Out)
The fear of missing important information or interactions can make it hard to disconnect.
Solution: Schedule specific times to check emails and messages. Remember, truly urgent matters will find a way to reach you.

Lack of Support from Others

Coworkers or family members might not respect your need for uninterrupted focus time.

Solution: Clearly communicate the importance of focus time for your productivity. Negotiate specific times when you'll be available for interruptions.

Difficulty with Self-Control

It's easy to give in to the temptation of "just a quick check" of email or social media.

Solution: Use technology to support your goals. Website blockers and app-limiting tools can provide external control when your willpower falters.

Constant Connectivity Expectations

In some workplaces, there's an expectation of constant availability.

Solution: Discuss realistic response time expectations with your manager or team. Propose a system for truly urgent matters that respects everyone's focus time.

Mind Wandering

Even in a distraction-free environment, your own thoughts can be distracting.

Solution: Practice mindfulness techniques. When you notice your mind wandering, gently bring your attention back to the task at hand without self-judgment.

Strategies for Eliminating Digital Distractions

Digital distractions are among the most prevalent and challenging to manage. Here are some strategies to minimize their impact:

1. Turn Off Notifications: Disable non-essential notifications on your devices. This includes social media alerts, email notifications, and app updates.
2. UseWebsiteBlockers: Installwebsiteblockersorproductivity apps to restrict access to distracting websites during work periods. Examples include StayFocusd, Freedom, and Cold Turkey.
3. Set Specific Times for Email: Allocate specific times for checking and responding to emails rather than constantly monitoring your inbox.
4. Limit Social Media Use: Set boundaries for social media usage. Use tools like Screen Time (iOS) or Digital Wellbeing (Android) to track and limit your usage.
5. Create a Digital Declutter Routine: Regularly organize and clean up your digital workspace, including files, emails, and apps.

Strategies for Minimizing Environmental Distractions

Creating a distraction-free environment can significantly enhance your focus and productivity. Here's how:

1. Designate a Workspace: Create a dedicated workspace that is free from distractions. This can be a home office, a quiet room, or a specific desk.

2. Use Noise-Canceling Tools: Invest in noise-canceling headphones or use white noise apps to block out background noise.
3. Set Boundaries: Communicate with family members or colleagues about your work hours and the importance of minimizing interruptions during those times.
4. Declutter Your Space: Keep your workspace clean and organized to reduce visual distractions. A clutter-free environment promotes mental clarity.
5. Control the Environment: Adjust lighting, temperature, and other environmental factors to create a comfortable and conducive work setting.

Strategies for Managing Internal Distractions

Internal distractions, such as intrusive thoughts and mental fatigue, can be challenging to manage. Here are some strategies to address them:

1. Practice Mindfulness: Incorporate mindfulness techniques, such as meditation or deep breathing exercises, to improve focus and reduce mental clutter.
2. Take Regular Breaks: Schedule regular breaks to rest and recharge. Short breaks help prevent burnout and maintain mental clarity.
3. WriteItDown:Ifyou'redistractedbythoughtsorworries, write them down and address them later. This helps clear your mind and refocus on the task at hand.
4. Set Clear Goals: Define clear, achievable goals for each work session to maintain focus and direction.
5. Prioritize Self-Care: Ensure you're getting enough sleep,

exercise, and healthy nutrition. A well-balanced lifestyle supports better concentration and productivity.

Techniques to Minimize Task Switching

Frequent task switching, also known as multitasking, can reduce productivity and increase errors. Here's how to minimize it:

1. Batch Similar Tasks: Group similar tasks together and complete them in dedicated time blocks. For example, handle all your emails in one session rather than sporadically throughout the day.
2. Use the Pomodoro Technique: Work in focused intervals (Pomodoros) with short breaks in between. This technique helps maintain concentration and reduce task switching.
3. Set Priorities: Use tools like the Eisenhower Matrix to prioritize tasks and focus on high-priority items first.
4. Limit Open Tabs: Keep only necessary tabs and applications open on your computer to avoid the temptation to switch tasks.
5. Create a Task List: Maintain a to-do list and check off tasks as you complete them. This visual progress tracker helps you stay focused on one task at a time.

Here are some additional real-life scenarios illustrating the elimination of distractions that will help you understand the chapter better.

Samantha, a remote worker, found herself constantly distracted by social media and household chores. She turned off notifications on her phone, set specific times for checking social media, and created a designated home office. By setting clear boundaries with her family and organizing her workspace, Samantha significantly reduced distractions and improved her productivity.

David, a college student, struggled with digital distractions while studying. He installed a website blocker to restrict access to social media during study sessions and used noise-canceling headphones to block out background noise. David also practiced mindfulness techniques to manage internal distractions and maintain focus on his studies.

Rachel, an entrepreneur, faced frequent interruptions from emails and team members. She set specific times for checking emails, communicated her work hours to her team, and used the Pomodoro Technique to maintain focus on high-priority tasks. By batching similar tasks and minimizing task switching, Rachel was able to stay productive and achieve her business goals.

> *"You can't depend on your eyes when your imagination is out of focus."*
> *– Mark Twain*

Techniques to Sustain Focus and Minimize Interruptions

To sustain focus and minimize interruptions, consider incorporating these techniques:

1. Create a Routine: Establish a daily routine that includes dedicated work periods, breaks, and personal time. Consistency helps reinforce focus and productivity.
2. Use Visual Cues: Use visual cues, such as "Do Not Disturb" signs or a timer, to signal to others and yourself that you're in a focused work period.
3. Limit Meetings: Reduce the number of meetings and ensure they are concise and purposeful. Schedule meetings during designated times to avoid interrupting focused work periods.
4. Practice Single-Tasking: Focus on completing one task at a time rather than multitasking. This improves the quality of your work and reduces errors.
5. Reflect and Adjust: Regularly reflect on your progress and identify any new distractions that arise. Adjust your strategies as needed to maintain a distraction-free environment.

Eliminating distractions and minimizing interruptions are essential steps in overcoming procrastination and boosting productivity. By identifying and systematically eliminating distractions, you're not just improving your productivity – you're reclaiming your attention and, by extension, your time and energy. This is a crucial step in overcoming procrastination and achieving your goals.

Remember, becoming distraction-free is a process, not an overnight transformation. Be patient with yourself as you implement these strategies. Remember, the key to success lies in maintaining discipline and consistency. With practice, you can develop habits that support sustained focus and productivity.

Are you ready to eliminate distractions and take control of your work environment for maximum productivity?

> *"Focus on the journey, not the destination. Joy is found not in finishing an activity but in doing it." – Greg Anderson*

7

Building Self-Discipline: Develop Good Habits

"Motivation gets you going, but discipline keeps you growing."
– John C. Maxwell

Self-discipline is the cornerstone of productivity and success. It is the ability to stay focused on your goals, manage your time effectively, and consistently make choices that align with your long-term objectives. Developing self-discipline requires building good habits that support your efforts to overcome procrastination. In this chapter, we'll explore strategies for building self-discipline and developing habits that lead to sustained productivity and success.

Building self-discipline and developing good habits are fundamental to overcoming procrastination and achieving long-term success. As the ancient Greek philosopher Aristotle once said, "We are what we repeatedly do. Excellence, then, is not an act, but a habit."

Understanding Self-Discipline

Self-discipline is the ability to control one's feelings and overcome weaknesses. It's about doing what needs to be done when it needs to be done, whether you feel like it or not. Self-discipline is the bridge between goals and accomplishments. Self-discipline is the practice of self-control. It involves the ability to resist short-term temptations in favor of long-term benefits. Unlike motivation, which can be fleeting, self-discipline is a consistent force that drives you to stay committed to your goals even when motivation wanes.

Key Components of Self-Discipline:

1. Commitment: A strong dedication to your goals and the willingness to make sacrifices to achieve them.
2. Consistency: The ability to maintain regular effort and focus over time.
3. Self-Control: Thecapacitytomanageimpulsesandresist distractions.
4. Persistence: The determination to keep going despite challenges and setbacks.

> *"Discipline is the bridge between goals and accomplishment."*
> *– Jim Rohn*

Strategies for Building Self-Discipline

Start Small
Don't try to overhaul your entire life overnight. Begin with small, manageable changes.
Example: If you want to develop a habit of early rising, start by setting your alarm just 15 minutes earlier than usual.

Be Consistent
Consistency is key in habit formation. Aim to perform your new habit at the same time each day.

Use the "If-Then" Technique
Create specific plans for implementing your habit using the format "If X happens, then I will do Y."
Example: "If it's 7 AM, then I will meditate for 10 minutes."

Practice Mindfulness
Mindfulness can increase your awareness of your thoughts and actions, making it easier to make conscious choices.

Remove Temptations
Make it easier to stick to your goals by removing potential distractions or temptations from your environment.

Forgive Yourself and Move Forward
Everyone slips up sometimes. Instead of berating yourself, acknowledge the lapse and immediately get back on track.

Visualize Success

Regularly visualize yourself successfully performing your new habit and enjoying its benefits.

Track Your Progress
Use a habit tracker or journal to monitor your progress. This provides motivation and accountability.

The Importance of Developing Good Habits

Good habits are the building blocks of self-discipline. They are automatic behaviors that support your goals and make it easier to stay on track. By developing positive habits, you reduce the need for constant willpower and create a structured routine that fosters productivity.

> *"We are what we repeatedly do. Excellence, then, is not an act, but a habit."*
> *– Aristotle*

Developing Good Habits

Here are some powerful habits that can significantly boost your productivity and help overcome procrastination:

Morning Routine
Develop a consistent morning routine to start your day right. This might include exercise, meditation, and reviewing your goals.

Time Blocking

Schedule specific blocks of time for different tasks or types of work.

Regular Breaks
Incorporate regular breaks into your day to maintain energy and focus.

Mindful Technology Use
Be intentional about when and how you use technology to avoid digital distractions.

Reflection and Planning
End each day with a brief period of reflection on what you've accomplished and planning for the next day.

Continuous Learning
Dedicate time each week to learning new skills or knowledge relevant to your goals.

Physical Exercise
Regular physical activity can boost energy, reduce stress, and improve cognitive function.

Let's see how these principles might work in practice. Sarah wants to improve her self-discipline to boost her productivity. Here's how she implements these strategies:
Week 1: Sarah starts small by committing to wake up 30 minutes earlier each day. She uses this time to meditate for 10 minutes and review her goals for the day.
Week 2: She implements time blocking, scheduling specific times for checking emails, meetings, and focused work.

Week 3: Sarah starts tracking her habits using a simple app. Seeing her streak of successful days motivates her to continue.

Week 4: She removes social media apps from her phone to reduce digital distractions during work hours.

Week 5: Sarah starts a regular exercise routine, going for a 30-minute walk during her lunch break.

Week 6: She begins ending each day with a 10-minute reflection and planning session for the next day.

Over time, these small changes compound, significantly improving Sarah's self-discipline and productivity.

Overcoming Common Self-Discipline Challenges

Building self-discipline isn't always easy. Here are some common challenges and how to address them:

Lack of Motivation
Some days, you just don't feel like putting in the effort.
Solution: Focus on your "why." Regularly remind yourself of the reasons behind your goals and the benefits of your new habits.

Inconsistency
It's easy to fall back into old patterns, especially when stressed or tired.
Solution: Use habit stacking – link your new habit to an existing one to increase consistency. For example, "After I brush my teeth, I will meditate for 10 minutes."

Impatience
Building self-discipline takes time, and it's easy to get

discouraged if you don't see immediate results.

Solution: Focus on the process, not just the outcome. Celebrate small wins along the way.

Environmental Factors

Your environment can make it harder to stick to your goals.

Solution: Shape your environment to support your goals. This might mean reorganizing your workspace, finding a workout buddy, or meal-prepping to support healthy eating habits.

All-or-Nothing Thinking

The belief that you've "ruined" your progress if you slip up once can lead to giving up entirely.

Solution: Embrace the "never miss twice" rule. If you miss a day, simply get back on track immediately the next day.

Benefits of Good Habits:

1. Increased Productivity: Good habits streamline your actions and make you more efficient.
2. Reduced Stress: Habits create a sense of order and predictability, reducing stress and anxiety.
3. Improved Health: Positive habits, such as regular exercise and healthy eating, contribute to overall well-being.
4. Enhanced Focus: Habits help you maintain focus and avoid distractions.
5. Long-Term Success: Consistent good habits lead to sustained progress and long-term success.

Here are some real-life scenarios illustrating the development of self-discipline and good habits:

John, an entrepreneur, struggled with time management and procrastination. He set a goal to improve his productivity by developing the habit of planning his day each morning. John started by dedicating 10 minutes every morning to plan his tasks and set priorities. Over time, this habit became ingrained, and he noticed a significant improvement in his productivity and focus.

Abby wanted to develop the habit of regular exercise. She started small by committing to a 10-minute workout every day. As she built consistency, she gradually increased the duration and intensity of her workouts. Abby used a habit-tracking app to monitor her progress and rewarded herself with a treat for every week she completed her workouts. This positive reinforcement kept her motivated and disciplined.

David, a college student, aimed to improve his study habits. He set a goal to study for 30 minutes every evening. David created a designated study space, eliminated distractions, and used a timer to keep himself accountable. By sticking to his routine, David developed strong study habits and noticed an improvement in his academic performance.

> *"The chains of habit are too weak to be felt until they are too strong to be broken."*
> *– Samuel Johnson*

Building self-discipline and developing good habits is not about perfection – it's about consistent progress. As author

James Clear puts it, "You do not rise to the level of your goals. You fall to the level of your systems."

By focusing on creating robust systems of self-discipline and positive habits, you're setting yourself up for long-term success in overcoming procrastination and achieving your goals. Remember, every small choice you make is shaping your future self.

As you move forward, choose one habit you'd like to develop and commit to practicing it consistently for the next 30 days. Use the strategies we've discussed to support your efforts. Remember, the journey of a thousand miles begins with a single step – or in this case, a single habit.

Are you ready to build self-discipline and develop good habits to achieve your goals and boost your productivity?

8

Overcoming Fear and Anxiety: Face YourFears

"Do the thing you fear, and the death of fear is certain."
– Ralph Waldo Emerson

Fear and anxiety are powerful emotions that can significantly impact productivity and contribute to procrastination. These emotions often stem from a fear of failure, fear of the unknown, or a lack of confidence. Overcoming fear and anxiety is crucial for achieving your goals and leading a fulfilling life. In this chapter, we'll explore strategies for identifying, confronting, and managing fear and anxiety to help you take control and move forward with confidence.

Understanding Fear and Anxiety

Fear and anxiety are natural responses to perceived threats. While fear is a reaction to an immediate danger, anxiety is a more generalized feeling of apprehension about potential future threats. Both emotions can be paralyzing and prevent you from taking action.

As the author Susan Jeffers famously said, "Feel the fear and do it anyway." This powerful mantra reminds us that fear doesn't have to be a stop sign; it can be a stepping stone to growth.

"Fear is only as deep as the mind allows." – Japanese Proverb

Common Sources of Fear and Anxiety:

1. Fear of Failure: Worrying about making mistakes or not meeting expectations.
2. Fear of the Unknown: Anxiety about uncertain outcomes or new experiences.
3. Fear of Judgment: Concern about how others perceive you or your actions.
4. Lack of Confidence: Doubts about your abilities or worthiness.
5. Past Experiences: Negative experiences that influence your current mindset.

The Impact of Fear and Anxiety on Productivity

Fear and anxiety can lead to several negative outcomes that hinder productivity:

1. Procrastination: Delaying tasks to avoid facing fears or discomfort.
2. Indecision: Struggling to make decisions due to fear of making the wrong choice.
3. Avoidance: Avoiding tasks or situations that trigger anxiety.
4. Low Motivation: Feeling demotivated and disengaged from work.
5. ReducedPerformance: Decreasedfocusandperformance due to mental distractions.

Strategies for Overcoming Fear and Anxiety

Practice Mindfulness:
Mindfulness can help you observe your fears without being overwhelmed by them. It creates a space between the fear and your reaction to it.
  Exercise: Try the STOP technique
  - S: Stop what you're doing
  - T: Take a breath
  - O: Observe your thoughts and feelings
  - P: Proceed with awareness

Challenge Your Thoughts:
  Often, our fears are based on irrational or exaggerated

thoughts. Question these thoughts and look for evidence that contradicts them.

> Exercise: Use the Triple Column Technique Column 1: Write down your fearful thought Column 2: Identify the cognitive distortion (e.g., catastro-

phizing, black-and-white thinking)

> Column 3: Write a more balanced, realistic thought

Gradual Exposure:

Facing your fears in small, manageable steps can help you build confidence over time.

> Exercise: Create a Fear Ladder

List your fear-inducing situations from least to most scary. Start by exposing yourself to the least scary situation and gradually work your way up.

Visualize Success:

Positive visualization can help counteract anxiety and build confidence.

> Exercise: Spend 5 minutes each day visualizing yourself successfully completing the task you've been avoiding.

Embrace Imperfection:

Perfectionism is often a major source of procrastination-inducing anxiety. Learn to embrace "good enough."

Exercise: Set a timer for a task and commit to submitting whatever you've completed when the timer goes off, even if it's not perfect.

Reframe Failure:

View failures as learning opportunities rather than personal deficiencies.

Exercise: After a setback, ask yourself, "What can I learn from this?" and "How can I use this experience to improve?"

Practice Self-Compassion:

Be kind to yourself when facing fears. Treat yourself with the same compassion you'd offer a good friend.

Exercise: Write a letter to yourself from the perspective of a supportive friend, offering encouragement about the situation you're facing.

Let's see how these strategies might work in practice. Mark has been avoiding giving presentations at work due to his fear of public speaking. Here's how he applies these techniques:

Mindfulness: Mark starts practicing daily meditation to become more aware of his anxiety symptoms without being overwhelmed by them.

Challenging Thoughts: He identifies his fearful thought, "I'll make a fool of myself and ruin my career," as catastrophizing. He reframes it to, "I might make some mistakes, but that's normal and won't define my entire career."

Gradual Exposure: Mark creates a fear ladder:

- Record himself giving a presentation alone
- Present to a close colleague
- Present to his small team
- Present at the department meeting
- Present at the company-wide meeting

Visualization: Each day, Mark spends 5 minutes visualizing himself confidently delivering a successful presentation.

Embracing Imperfection: He commits to giving his first team presentation without aiming for perfection, focusing instead on clear communication.

Reframing Failure: After his first presentation, Mark notes areas for improvement without harsh self-judgment, viewing them as learning opportunities.

Self-Compassion: He writes himself a supportive letter, acknowledging his courage in facing his fear and encouraging continued growth.

Over time, Mark's fear of public speaking diminishes, and he becomes more confident in his presentation skills.

> *"You gain strength, courage, and confidence by every experience in which you really stop to look fear in the face. You must do the thing you think you cannot do."*
> *– Eleanor Roosevelt*

Overcoming Common Challenges in Facing Fears

Even with these strategies, overcoming fears can be challenging. Herearesomecommonobstaclesandhowtoaddress them:

Avoidance Behaviors:
It's easy to fall back into avoiding fear-inducing situations.

Solution: Create accountability. Share your goals with a trusted friend or mentor who can encourage you to stay on track.

Overwhelming Anxiety:
Sometimes, anxiety can feel too intense to manage. Solution: Use grounding techniques like deep breathing or the 5-4-3-2-1 method (identify 5 things you can see, 4 you can touch, 3 you can hear, 2 you can smell, and 1 you can taste).

Setbacks:
   Progress isn't always linear. Setbacks can be discouraging.
   Solution: Expect and plan for setbacks. View them as part of the learning process rather than failures.

Negative Self-Talk:
   Our inner critic can be loud when we're facing fears.
   Solution: Practice positive self-talk. Create a list of encouraging phrases to counter negative thoughts.

Comparison to Others:
   Comparing your progress to others can fuel anxiety.
   Solution: Focus on your own journey. Keep a progress journal to remind yourself how far you've come.

Here are some real-life scenarios illustrating how individuals have overcome fear and anxiety:

   Lisa had a fear of public speaking that hindered her career progress. She decided to confront her fear by joining a local Toastmasters club. Through regular practice, feedback, and gradual exposure to speaking in front of an audience, Lisa built her confidence and overcame her fear. Today, she speaks at conferences and leads workshops with ease.

Mike, a recent college graduate, felt anxious about job interviews and feared rejection. He addressed his anxiety by researching common interview questions, practicing with friends, and using relaxation techniques before interviews. By preparing thoroughly and facing his fears, Mike gained confidence and secured a job in his desired field.

Rachel wanted to start her own business but was paralyzed by the fear of failure. She sought support from a mentor and joined a local entrepreneur group. By setting small, achievable goals and celebrating each milestone, Rachel gradually built her business and overcame her fear of failure.

> *"The only thing we have to fear is fear itself." –*
> *Franklin D. Roosevelt*

Overcoming fear and anxiety is not about eliminating these emotions entirely – it's about learning to move forward despite them. By identifying your fears, challenging negative thoughts, and using effective coping strategies, you can take control and move forward with confidence. As author Ambrose Redmoon said, "Courage is not the absence of fear, but rather the judgment that something else is more important than fear."

By facing your fears, you're not just overcoming procrastination – you're expanding your comfort zone and opening yourself up to new opportunities for growth and success. Remember, every time you face a fear, you're building resilience and self-confidence that will serve you well in all areas of life. With dedication and the right support, you can overcome fear and anxiety, leading to increased productivity and personal growth.

Are you ready to face your fears and take control of your life, overcoming anxiety and moving confidently towards your goals?

9

Creating a Conducive Work Environment: Optimize Your Space

"Your environment influences your mindset, and your mindset determines your success."
– *Unknown*

Your work environment plays a crucial role in your productivity and overall well-being. A well-organized and conducive workspace can significantly enhance focus, creativity, and efficiency, while a cluttered or distracting environment can lead to procrastination and stress. In this chapter, we will explore strategies for optimizing your workspace to create a productive and inspiring atmosphere that supports your goals.

The Importance of a Conducive Work Environment

Your work environment affects you in more ways than you might realize. It influences your mood, energy levels, focus, and ultimately, your productivity. As the famous architect Winston Churchill once said, "We shape our buildings; thereafter they shape us." The same principle applies to our workspaces, whether that's an office, a home study, or a corner of your living room.

A conducive work environment is one that minimizes distractions, promotes comfort, and supports efficient workflow. Key benefits include:

1. Enhanced Focus: A well-organized space reduces distractions, allowing for better concentration.
2. Increased Productivity: An optimized workspace promotes efficient task management and workflow.
3. Reduced Stress: A clean and comfortable environment can lower stress levels.
4. Improved Health: Ergonomic furniture and proper lighting can prevent physical strain and improve overall health.
5. BoostedCreativity: Aninspiringworkspacecanstimulate creativity and innovation.

Key Elements of a Conducive Work Environment

Lighting
Proper lighting is crucial for maintaining focus and preventing eye strain. Natural light is ideal, but if that's not possible, ensure your space is well-lit with artificial lighting that mimics natural light

Tip: Position your desk near a window if possible. If not,

consider using full-spectrum light bulbs.

Ergonomics

A comfortable, ergonomic setup can prevent physical discomfort and help you maintain focus for longer periods.

Key considerations:

- Chair: Should support your back and allow your feet to rest flat on the floor
- Desk: At a height where your elbows can rest at about 90 degrees
- Monitor: Top of the screen should be at or slightly below eye level
- Keyboard and mouse: Positioned to keep your wrists straight

Organization

A clutter-free environment can lead to a clutter-free mind. Organize your space to minimize distractions and maximize efficiency.

Tip: Implement the "one in, one out" rule. For every new item you bring into your workspace, remove one item.

Temperature

Studies show that the ideal temperature for productivity is between 70-77°F (21-25°C). Too hot or too cold can significantly impact your focus and energy levels.

Noise Level

While some people work well with background noise, for many, a quiet environment is crucial for deep focus. If you can't control external noise, consider using noise cancelling headphones.

Color
Colors can affect mood and productivity. Blue can enhance focus, yellow can boost creativity, and green can promote balance and harmony.

Tip: If you can't paint your walls, incorporate these colors through accessories or artwork.

Plants
Indoor plants can improve air quality, reduce stress, and increase productivity. Studies have shown that having plants in the workspace can increase productivity by up to 15%.

Personalization
While keeping clutter to a minimum, add personal touches that inspire and motivate you. This could be artwork, photos, or meaningful objects.

Creating Your Ideal Work Environment

Assess Your Current Space
Take a critical look at your current work environment. What's working? What isn't? Make a list of areas for improvement.

Declutter and Organize
Remove anything that doesn't contribute to your work or well-being. Organize remaining items efficiently.

Optimize Lighting
Maximize natural light if possible. If not, invest in good quality artificial lighting.

Ensure Ergonomic Comfort
Invest in an ergonomic chair and adjust your desk setup for optimal comfort.

Manage Noise
Create a quiet environment or use noise-cancelling headphones if necessary.

Control Temperature
Adjust heating/cooling for optimal comfort, or use a small fan or heater if you can't control the overall temperature.

Add Plants
Introduce one or two low-maintenance plants to your workspace.

Personalize Thoughtfully
Add a few inspiring or motivating personal touches without creating clutter.

Let's see how these principles might work in practice. Sarah, a freelance graphic designer, decides to optimize her home office:

1. Assessment: Sarah realizes her current setup has poor lighting, is cluttered, and her chair is uncomfortable.
2. Decluttering: She removes unnecessary items, keeping

only essential tools and a few inspirational objects.
3. Lighting: Sarah moves her desk near the window and adds a desk lamp with adjustable brightness.
4. Ergonomics: She invests in an ergonomic chair and adjusts her monitor height.
5. Organization: Sarah implements a filing system for documents and a cable management solution.
6. Plants: She adds a low-maintenance snake plant to her desk.
7. Color: Sarah incorporates blue accents through a desk organizer and artwork to enhance focus.
8. Personalization: She hangs a small bulletin board with inspirational quotes and photos of completed projects.

After these changes, Sarah finds she's more focused, comfortable, and productive in her new workspace.

> *"Clutter is not just the stuff on your floor—it's anything that stands between you and the life you want to be living." – Peter Walsh*

Overcoming Common Organizing Workspace Challenges

Even with the best intentions, creating an ideal work environment can be challenging. Here are some common issues and how to address them:

Limited Space
Not everyone has a dedicated office or even a large workspace.

Solution: Get creative with multi-functional furniture. A fold-down desk or a room divider can create a "work zone" even in a small space.

Shared Spaces

If you share your workspace with others, it can be hard to control all elements.

Solution: Use noise-cancelling headphones, a privacy screen, or consider alternating work hours if possible.

Budget Constraints

Creating an ideal workspace can seem expensive.
Solution: Prioritize the most important elements (like an ergonomic chair) and look for budget-friendly alternatives for other items.

Distracting Home Environment

Working from home can come with its own set of distractions.

Solution: Establish clear boundaries with family members or roommates. Use visual cues (like a "Do Not Disturb" sign) to signal when you're in work mode.

Lack of Motivation in the Space

Sometimes, even a well-designed space can feel uninspiring.
Solution: Regularly refresh your space with small changes. Rotate artwork, rearrange items, or introduce a new plant to keep the environment feeling fresh.

Here are some real-life examples of individuals who have optimized their workspaces:

Alex, a remote worker, struggled with distractions and discomfort in his home office. He invested in an ergonomic chair, positioned his desk near a window for natural light, and used a cable management system to declutter his workspace. By incorporating plants and personal items, Alex created a comfortable and productive environment that improved his focus and efficiency.

Emily, a graphic designer, needed a workspace that inspired creativity. She added colorful artwork, a vision board, and a variety of plants to her office. Emily also used task lighting and ergonomic furniture to create a functional and inspiring workspace. Her optimized environment boosted her creativity and productivity.

James, an entrepreneur, needed a highly organized workspace to manage multiple projects. He implemented a filing system, used productivity apps to track tasks, and created designated zones for different activities. By optimizing his workspace, James improved his efficiency and reduced stress.

> *"A room should never allow the eye to settle in one place. It should smile at you and create fantasy."*
> *– Juan Montoya*

Techniques to Maintain a Conducive Work Environment

To maintain a conducive work environment, consider incorporating these techniques:

1. Regular Maintenance: Schedule regular cleaning and decluttering sessions to keep your workspace organized.
2. Adjust as Needed: Continuously assess and adjust your workspace to meet your changing needs and preferences.
3. Stay Flexible: Be willing to experiment with different layouts and setups to find what works best for you.
4. IncorporateBreaks: Includeregularbreaksinyourschedule to rest and recharge. A well-rested mind is more productive and creative.
5. SetBoundaries: Establishclearboundariesbetweenwork and personal life to maintain a healthy work-life balance.

Creating a conducive work environment is essential for enhancing productivity, reducing stress, and achieving your goals. By focusing on ergonomics, lighting, organization, personalization, and technology, you can optimize your workspace to support your efforts and inspire success. Remember, your work environment should evolve with your needs and preferences, so be open to making adjustments and improvements. With a well-designed workspace, you can boost your productivity and create an atmosphere that fosters growth and creativity.

Remember, the perfect work environment looks different for everyone. What matters is that your space works for you, supporting your unique work style and goals. As you implement changes, pay attention to how they affect your mood, energy levels, and productivity. Be willing to experiment and adjust until you find your optimal setup.

As you move forward, choose one aspect of your work environment to improve this week. Whether it's decluttering your desk, adjusting your lighting, or adding a plant, take that first step towards creating a space that inspires and motivates you.

Are you ready to optimize your workspace and create a conducive environment that supports your productivity and success?

10

Getting Accountability: Find a Study Buddy

"Accountability breeds response-ability."
- Stephen Covey

Procrastination often thrives in isolation. When we're alone with our tasks, it's easy to succumb to distractions or convince ourselves that we can always start "later." This is where the power of accountability comes in, and one of the most effective forms of accountability is finding a study buddy. In this chapter, we'll explore how partnering up can revolutionize your productivity and help you overcome procrastination.

The Power of Accountability

Accountability is a powerful tool for overcoming procrastination and achieving your goals. Accountability involves taking responsibility for your actions and being answerable to someone else. When you know that someone else is aware of your goals and is monitoring your progress, you are more likely to stay committed and take consistent action.

Psychologist Dr. Gail Matthews conducted a study on goal achievement and found that people who wrote down their goals, shared them with others, and sent weekly updates to their friends were 33% more successful in accomplishing their goals than those who merely formulated goals without sharing them.

> *"Accountability is the glue that ties commitment to the result." – Bob Proctor*

Benefits of Accountability:

1. Increased Motivation: Knowing that someone else is watching your progress can boost your motivation to stay on track.
2. Improved Focus: Regular check-ins with an accountability partner help you maintain focus and avoid distractions.
3. Enhanced Commitment: Sharing your goals with someone else reinforces your commitment to achieving them.
4. Mutual Support: An accountability partner provides encouragement, feedback, and support during challenging times.
5. Shared Resources: Collaborating with a study buddy allows you to share knowledge, resources, and study techniques.

Finding Your Ideal Study Buddy

Now that we understand the importance of accountability, let's focus on finding the right study buddy. Your study buddy doesn't necessarily have to be studying the same subject as you. The key is to find someone who is also committed to improving their productivity and overcoming procrastination.

Here are some places to look for a potential study buddy:

1. Classmates or coworkers
2. Online forums or social media groups focused on productivity
3. Friends or family members with similar goals
4. Local meetup groups or community centers
5. Study buddy matching websites or apps

When choosing a study buddy, consider the following qualities:

Reliability: Your study buddy should be someone who consistently shows up and follows through on commitments.

Similar goals: While you don't need to have identical objectives, having similar aspirations can help you understand and support each other better.

Complementary strengths: Look for someone whose strengths complement your weaknesses and vice versa.

Positive attitude: A study buddy with a can-do attitude can help motivate you during challenging times.

Good communication skills: Open and honest communication is crucial for a successful accountability partnership.

Sarah, a medical student, was struggling with procrastination while preparing for her board exams. She decided to find a study buddy and connected with Mike, a law student preparing for the bar exam. Despite their different fields, they both shared the goal of improving their study habits and overcoming procrastination.

They set up regular check-ins, shared their weekly goals, and reported their progress to each other. Sarah found that knowing Mike was expecting an update motivated her to stay on track. Similarly, Mike felt more accountable knowing that Sarah would ask about his progress.

Within a month, both Sarah and Mike noticed significant improvements in their productivity. Sarah's practice test scores improved, and Mike found himself consistently meeting his study targets. Their partnership not only helped them overcome procrastination but also provided mutual support during stressful times.

Establishing an Effective Study Buddy System

Once you've found your study buddy, it's essential to establish a system that works for both of you. Here are some key elements to consider:

Set Clear Goals and Expectations
Begin by clearly defining what each of you hopes to achieve through this partnership. Discuss your individual goals, the areas where you struggle with procrastination, and what you expect from each other as accountability partners.

Establish Regular Check-ins

Decide on a schedule for your check-ins. This could be daily, weekly, or bi-weekly, depending on your needs and availability. Consistency is key, so choose a frequency that you can both commit to.

Choose Your Communication Method

Determine how you'll communicate. This could be through:
- In-person meetings
- Video calls
- Phone calls
- Text messages
- Email updates

Choose a method that works best for both of you and stick to it.

Create a Progress Tracking System

Develop a system to track your progress. This could be a shared spreadsheet, a collaborative task management app, or simply a notebook where you both record your goals and achievements.

Implement Consequences and Rewards

Consider establishing friendly consequences for missed targets and rewards for achieving goals. This adds an element of fun and extra motivation to your accountability system.

> *"Motivation is what gets you started. Habit is what keeps you going."*
> *- Jim Rohn*

Maximizing Your Study Buddy Relationship

To get the most out of your study buddy partnership, consider implementing these strategies:

Be Honest and Transparent

Open communication is crucial. Be honest about your struggles and successes. If you're having a hard time meeting your goals, don't hide it from your study buddy. They're there to support you, not judge you.

Offer Support and Encouragement

Remember that this is a two-way relationship. Be there to support and encourage your study buddy, just as they support you. Celebrate each other's successes, no matter how small.

Share Techniques and Resources

Exchange productivity tips, study techniques, and useful resources. You might discover new strategies that work well for you.

Hold Each Other Accountable, But Be Understanding

While it's important to hold each other accountable, remember to be understanding if your study buddy occasionally falls short. Life happens, and a good accountability partner offers support during challenging times.

Regularly Reassess and Adjust

As you progress, your needs and goals may change. Regularly reassess your study buddy system and make adjustments as necessary to ensure it continues to be effective for both of you.

Let's consider another example. Tom, a freelance writer, struggled with procrastination when working on his first novel. He lived in a small town and couldn't find a local study buddy, so he turned to an online writing forum. There, he connected with three other aspiring novelists from different parts of the world.

They formed a virtual study group, meeting weekly via video call to discuss their progress, share excerpts of their work, and set goals for the coming week. They also created a shared online document where they logged their daily word counts.

The group's diverse perspectives and shared passion for writing created a motivating environment. Tom found that the regular check-ins and the knowledge that his group members were expecting to see his progress pushed him to write consistently, even on days when he didn't feel inspired.

Within six months, Tom had completed the first draft of his novel, a feat he attributes largely to the accountability provided by his virtual study group.

Overcoming Common Challenges

While having a study buddy can be incredibly beneficial, it's not without its challenges. Here are some common issues you might face and how to address them:

Mismatched Commitment Levels
If you find that you and your study buddy have different levels of commitment, have an honest conversation about your

expectations and goals. If the mismatch is too great, it might be best to find a new partner.

Schedule Conflicts

Life can get busy, making it difficult to maintain regular check-ins. Be flexible and willing to adjust your schedule. Consider using asynchronous communication methods like email or voice messages if real-time meetings become challenging.

Loss of Motivation

If either you or your study buddy start losing motivation, try mixing things up. Change your meeting format, set new types of goals, or introduce new accountability methods to reignite your enthusiasm.

Dependency

While accountability is helpful, be careful not to become overly dependent on your study buddy. The goal is to develop self-discipline and intrinsic motivation alongside external accountability.

> *"The only person you are destined to become is the person you decide to be."*
> *- Ralph Waldo Emerson*

Here are some real-life examples of successful study partnerships:

Maria and John, university students studying for their final exams, decided to become study buddies. They created a study schedule, divided the subjects between them, and held weekly study sessions. By sharing notes, discussing difficult topics, and quizzing each other, they both improved their understanding and performed well in their exams.

Alex and Sam were preparing for a professional certification exam. They found each other through an online forum and decided to partner up. They set specific goals, created a detailed study plan, and held virtual study sessions twice a week. Their partnership provided mutual support, motivation, and accountability, leading to their successful certification.

Sophie and Liam wanted to improve their Spanish skills. They met through a language learning app and decided to practice together. They set goals to have weekly conversations in Spanish, share vocabulary lists, and review grammar. Their consistent practice and mutual encouragement significantly enhanced their language proficiency.

> *"Surround yourself with only people who are going to lift you higher."*
> *– Oprah Winfrey*

Finding a study buddy and establishing a system of mutual accountability can be a game-changer in your battle against procrastination. By leveraging the power of social commitment and support, you create an environment that nurtures productivity and personal growth.

Remember, the journey to overcoming procrastination is not always smooth, but with a reliable study buddy by your side, you'll have the support and motivation to push through challenges and achieve your goals. Whether you're writing a novel, studying for exams, or working on personal development, a study buddy can be the catalyst that transforms your intentions into actions and your dreams into reality.

As you move forward, embrace the power of accountability. Reach out, connect, and partner up. Your future, more productive self will thank you for taking this important step in conquering procrastination.

Are you ready to find a study buddy and harness the power of accountability to boost your productivity and achieve your goals?

> *"Alone we can do so little; together we can do so much."*
> *– Helen Keller*

11

Rewarding Progress: Celebrate Small Wins

"Celebrate what you want to see more of."
– Tom Peters

In the journey to achieve your goals, recognizing and celebrating small wins is essential. These small victories provide motivation, boost morale, and keep you on track. Celebrating progress helps reinforce positive behavior and makes the pursuit of larger goals more enjoyable. In this chapter, we will explore the importance of rewarding progress, different ways to celebrate small wins, and how to integrate these celebrations into your daily routine to maintain momentum and stay motivated.

The Importance of Celebrating Small Wins
Celebrating small wins is crucial for several reasons:

1. Boosts Motivation: Recognizing progress provides a sense of accomplishment, which fuels motivation to continue working towards your goals.
2. Reinforces Positive Behavior: Celebrating achievements reinforces the behaviors and actions that led to success, encouraging you to repeat them.
3. Builds Confidence: Each small win enhances your confidence and belief in your ability to achieve your larger goals.
4. Reduces Burnout: Regularly celebrating progress prevents burnout by breaking up the monotony of long-term efforts with moments of joy and satisfaction.
5. Creates Momentum: Small wins build momentum, making it easier to tackle subsequent tasks and challenges.

> *"Big things are built one brick at a time. Victories are achieved one choice at a time. A life well-lived is chosen one day at a time."*
> *- Lysa TerKeurst*

Marie, an aspiring novelist, had been procrastinating on writing her book for years. Every time she sat down to write, she felt overwhelmed by the enormity of the task ahead. After learning about the power of small wins, she decided to change her approach.

Instead of focusing on completing the entire novel, Marie set a small, daily goal of writing just 300 words. Each time she met this goal, she would celebrate by treating herself to a favorite snack or taking a short walk in the park.

At first, the progress seemed minimal. But as the days went by, Marie found herself looking forward to her writing sessions and the small celebration that followed. Some days she even exceeded her goal, writing 500 or 600 words. After three months, she had consistently met her daily goal and had written over 27,000 words – more than she had managed in the previous three years combined.

Marie's story illustrates how celebrating small wins can transform a daunting task into a series of achievable goals, building momentum and motivation along the way.

Strategies for Identifying and Celebrating Small Wins

Now that we understand the importance of small wins, let's explore some strategies for identifying and celebrating them:

Break Down Large Goals
The first step in celebrating small wins is to create them. Break down your larger goals into smaller, manageable tasks. For instance, if your goal is to clean out your garage, break it down into smaller tasks like "sort through one box" or "clear one shelf."

Set Daily or Weekly Micro-Goals
Establish small, achievable goals for each day or week. These could be as simple as "spend 15 minutes on project X" or

"complete two items on my to-do list."

Use a Progress Tracking System
Implement a system to track your progress visually. This could be a habit tracker app, a wall calendar where you mark completed tasks, or a jar where you add a marble for each small win.

Acknowledge Effort, Not Just Outcomes
Remember to celebrate the effort you put in, not just the end results. If you've been procrastinating on a task for weeks and finally start working on it, that's a win worth celebrating, even if you haven't completed the task yet.

Create a Celebration Menu
Develop a list of small rewards or celebrations that you enjoy. These could include:
- Enjoying a favorite snack or beverage
- Taking a short walk or break
- Watching an episode of a favorite TV show
- Calling a friend to share your accomplishment
- Engaging in a hobby for a set amount of time

Make Celebrations Immediate and Consistent
Try to celebrate immediately after achieving a small win. Consistency is key – make celebration a habit to reinforce positive behavior.

Share Your Wins
Consider sharing your small wins with a supportive friend, family member, or online community. External validation can

provide an additional motivational boost.

> *"Success is the sum of small efforts, repeated day in and day out." - Robert Collier*

This quote reminds us that big achievements are often the result of consistent small efforts over time.

Overcoming Challenges in Celebrating Small Wins

While the concept of celebrating small wins is simple, implementing it consistently can be challenging. Here are some common obstacles and how to overcome them:

Feeling Like Your Wins Are Too Small to Celebrate
Sometimes, we might feel that our accomplishments are too insignificant to warrant celebration. Remember, what matters is progress, not the size of the step. Even tiny steps forward are moving you away from procrastination and towards your goals.

Forgetting to Celebrate
In the busyness of life, it's easy to forget to acknowledge our small wins. Set reminders on your phone or computer, or use visual cues in your environment to prompt celebration.

Celebrations Feeling Forced or Insincere
   If celebrations feel artificial, experiment with different types of acknowledgment until you find what feels genuine to you. Sometimes, a simple moment of self-acknowledgment can be just as powerful as a more elaborate celebration.

Negative Self-Talk

Our inner critic can sometimes diminish our small wins. Practice self-compassion and remind yourself that every step forward, no matter how small, is progress.

Let us consider another example. Tom had been putting off getting in shape for years. Every January, he'd make a New Year's resolution to exercise regularly, but by February, his motivation would fizzle out. This year, he decided to try a different approach, focusing on small wins.

Instead of setting a vague goal to "get fit," Tom started with a tiny goal: put on his workout clothes every day after work. He celebrated each day he did this, regardless of whether he actually exercised, by putting a gold star on his calendar.

After a week of consistently changing into workout clothes, Tom added another small goal: do just one push-up. Again, he celebrated each day he met this goal.

Gradually, Tom increased his goals. One push-up became five, then ten. Putting on workout clothes led to taking a 5-minute walk, then a 10-minute jog. Each small win was celebrated, building Tom's confidence and motivation.

Six months later, Tom was exercising regularly, had lost weight, and felt more energetic. By focusing on and celebrating small wins, he built a sustainable fitness habit without ever feeling overwhelmed.

Different Ways to Celebrate Small Wins

Celebrating small wins doesn't have to be elaborate or expensive. Here are some simple and effective ways to reward yourself:

1. Treat Yourself: Reward yourself with something you enjoy, like a favorite snack, a new book, or a relaxing activity.

2. Take a Break: Give yourself a short break to relax and recharge. Enjoy a walk, meditate, or spend time with loved ones.

3. Share Your Success: Share your achievements with friends, family, or colleagues. Their positive feedback and encouragement can boost your morale.

4. Create a Visual Reminder: Use a visual tracker, like a progress chart or a vision board, to mark and celebrate milestones. Seeing your progress visually can be very motivating.

5. Celebrate with Others: Organize small celebrations with friends or colleagues. Group celebrations can enhance the sense of accomplishment and camaraderie.

6. Give Yourself Time: Allow yourself time to enjoy hobbies or activities you love. This can be a great way to reward yourself while also taking a break from work.

7. Set Up a Reward System: Create a reward system for yourself, where you earn points or rewards for completing tasks and reaching milestones.

"Progress is not always linear. Be patient with yourself and your progress. Every step forward is a step in the

> *right direction, no matter how small."*
> *– Unknown*

Cultivating a Small Wins Mindset

Ultimately, celebrating small wins is about more than just implementing a few strategies – it's about cultivating a mindset that values progress over perfection. Here are some tips for developing this mindset:

Practice Gratitude
Take time each day to appreciate the progress you've made, no matter how small. This helps shift your focus from what's left to do to what you've already accomplished.

Redefine Success
Instead of seeing success as a distant, final goal, start viewing it as a series of small achievements along the way.

Be Patient with Yourself
Remember that change takes time. Be patient and kind to yourself as you work on overcoming procrastination.

Learn from Setbacks
When you face setbacks (and you will), treat them as learning opportunities rather than failures. Celebrate the lessons learned.

Surround Yourself with Support
Share your small wins with supportive friends or join a community that values and celebrates progress.

Here are some real-life examples of how individuals celebrate their small wins:

Emily, a college student, sets weekly study goals. Every time she completes a study session, she treats herself to a small piece of chocolate and takes a 15-minute break to do something she enjoys. This simple reward system keeps her motivated and focused.

James, a marketing professional, tracks his project milestones using a digital tracker. When he reaches a significant milestone, he shares his success with his team and treats himself to a coffee from his favorite café. Celebrating these wins helps him stay motivated and maintain a positive attitude.

Sarah, an entrepreneur, celebrates her business achievements by organizing small team gatherings. After launching a successful campaign or reaching a sales target, she takes her team out for a casual lunch. This not only rewards her hard work but also fosters team spirit and collaboration.

> *"The more you praise and celebrate your life, the more there is in life to celebrate." – Oprah Winfrey*

Techniques to Integrate Celebrations into Your Routine

To make celebrating small wins a regular part of your routine, consider these techniques:

1. Schedule Celebrations: Include time for celebrations in your calendar. This ensures you don't overlook the importance of recognizing progress.
2. Set Reminders: Use reminders or alarms to prompt you to reflect on your achievements and celebrate them regularly.

3. Create a Celebration Ritual: Develop a simple ritual for celebrating wins, such as lighting a candle, playing a favorite song, or writing a gratitude note.
4. Involve Others: Share your celebration plans with friends or family and invite them to join you. Their participation can make the experience more enjoyable and meaningful.
5. Stay Flexible: Be open to adjusting your celebration methods based on your needs and preferences. Flexibility ensures that the celebrations remain meaningful and effective.

Celebrating small wins is a powerful tool in the battle against procrastination. By breaking down large tasks into smaller, manageable steps and acknowledging our progress along the way, you can build momentum, boost motivation, and gradually overcome the tendency to procrastinate.

Remember, every giant leap is made up of many small steps. By celebrating these steps, you create a positive feedback loop that encourages you to keep moving forward. So, the next time you make even the tiniest bit of progress on a task you've been putting off, take a moment to acknowledge and celebrate it. Your future, more productive self will thank you for it.

As you move forward in your journey to overcome procrastination, make celebrating small wins a regular part of your routine. With time and consistency, you'll find that these small celebrations can lead to big changes in your productivity and overall sense of accomplishment.

Are you ready to start celebrating your small wins and harnessing the power of positive reinforcement to achieve your goals?

12

Building Resilience: Bounce Back from Failure

"Fall seven times, stand up eight."
– Japanese Proverb

Failure is an inevitable part of life, but how you respond to it makes all the difference. Resilience, the ability to bounce back from setbacks and persevere through challenges, is a crucial skill for personal and professional growth. Building resilience helps you overcome obstacles, learn from mistakes, and continue moving forward. In this chapter, we will explore the nature of resilience, strategies to develop it, and real-life examples of people who have successfully bounced back from failure.

Understanding Resilience

Resilience is not about avoiding failure but rather about how you handle it. It involves maintaining a positive outlook, adapting to change, and continuing to pursue your goals despite setbacks.

Key Aspects of Resilience:

1. Emotional Regulation: Managing your emotions in the face of adversity to stay focused and composed.
2. Optimism: Maintaining a positive outlook and believing in your ability to overcome challenges.
3. Self-Efficacy: Having confidence in your ability to solve problems and handle difficulties.
4. Adaptability: Being flexible and willing to adjust your approach when faced with obstacles.
5. Support Systems: Building strong relationships and seeking support from others during tough times.

> *"Resilience is not about being able to bounce back from a high, or to get through a challenging experience. It's about being able to bounce forward."*
> *- Sheryl Sandberg*

The Link Between Resilience and Procrastination

Procrastination often stems from a fear of failure or perfectionism. When we lack resilience, these fears can become paralyzing, leading us to put off tasks indefinitely. By building resilience, we develop the confidence to face potential failures and the ability to learn from our mistakes, reducing our tendency to procrastinate.

Let's see resilience in practice. Sarah, a graduate student, had been procrastinating on her thesis for months. Every time she sat down to write, she was overwhelmed by the fear that her work wouldn't be good enough. This fear led her to put off writing, creating a vicious cycle of procrastination and anxiety.

After learning about resilience, Sarah decided to change her approach. She started by setting small, achievable goals for her thesis work. When she faced setbacks, instead of seeing them as evidence of her inadequacy, she viewed them as opportunities to learn and improve.

Over time, Sarah developed more confidence in her ability to handle challenges. She became less afraid of potential failures and more focused on the process of learning and growing. As a result, her procrastination decreased, and she made steady progress on her thesis.

Strategies to Build Resilience

Developing resilience is a continuous process that involves adopting specific habits and mindsets. Here are some strategies to help you build resilience:
   Embrace Failure as a Learning Opportunity:
   View failures as valuable lessons rather than as setbacks. Each failure provides insights that can help you improve and grow.

Thomas Edison, who famously said, *"I have not failed. I've just found 10,000 ways that won't work"* viewed each failure as a step closer to success.

Cultivate a Growth Mindset:

Believe in your ability to develop and improve through effort and learning. A growth mindset helps you see challenges as opportunities to grow.

> *"Success is not final, failure is not fatal: It is the courage to continue that counts." – Winston Churchill*

Set Realistic Goals:

Break down larger goals into smaller, achievable tasks. This makes it easier to manage setbacks and maintain motivation.

J.K. Rowling faced numerous rejections before "Harry Potter" was published. She focused on her writing and took one step at a time, eventually achieving immense success.

Practice Self-Compassion:

Be kind to yourself when things don't go as planned. Self-compassion helps you recover from setbacks without being overly critical.

> *"You are imperfect, you are wired for struggle, but you are worthy of love and belonging." – Brené Brown*

Build Strong Relationships:

Surround yourself with supportive friends, family, and colleagues. A strong support network provides encouragement and assistance during difficult times.

Oprah Winfrey credits her support network, including mentors and friends, for helping her overcome numerous challenges in her career.

Maintain Perspective:

Keep setbacks in perspective and avoid catastrophic thinking. Remember that a single failure does not define your overall success.

> *"In the middle of difficulty lies opportunity."* – Albert Einstein

Develop Coping Strategies:

Learn and practice effective coping strategies, such as mindfulness, meditation, and physical exercise, to manage stress and maintain mental well-being.

Michael Jordan, considered one of the greatest basketball players of all time, was cut from his high school basketball team. He used this setback as motivation to work harder and improve his skills.

Overcoming Common Challenges in Building Resilience

Building resilience is a process that comes with its own set of challenges. Here are some common obstacles and how to overcome them:

Perfectionism

Perfectionism can hinder resilience by making us overly critical of our efforts.

Solution: Practice setting "good enough" goals. Recognize

that progress is more important than perfection.

Negative Self-Talk
Our internal dialogue can significantly impact our resilience.
Solution: Practice cognitive restructuring. Challenge negative thoughts and replace them with more balanced, realistic ones.

Fear of Failure
The fear of failing can prevent us from taking risks necessary for growth.
Solution: Reframe failure as a learning opportunity. Adopt a "fail forward" mentality, where each failure is seen as a step towards success.

Lack of Patience
Building resilience takes time, and it's easy to get discouraged if we don't see immediate results.
Solution: Focus on the process rather than the outcome. Celebrate small improvements and remember that progress is rarely linear.

> *"The greatest glory in living lies not in never falling,*
> *but in rising every time we fall."*
> *- Nelson Mandela*

Let me give you a few more examples relating to real-life scenarios so that it will help you understand resilience better.

Walt Disney faced numerous setbacks before creating the iconic Disney brand. He was fired from a newspaper job for lacking imagination, and his first animation company went bankrupt. Despite these failures, Disney persisted and eventually revolutionized the entertainment industry.

Harland Sanders, the founder of KFC, faced many rejections before achieving success. At the age of 65, he pitched his fried chicken recipe to over 1,000 restaurants before finding success. His persistence and resilience turned KFC into a global brand.

Malala Yousafzai, a Pakistani activist for female education, survived an assassination attempt by the Taliban. Despite this traumatic experience, she continued her advocacy work and became the youngest-ever Nobel Prize laureate. Her resilience and dedication have inspired millions worldwide.

> "Resilience is knowing that you are the only one that has the power and the responsibility to pick yourself up."
> – Mary Holloway

Building Resilience in Daily Life

Incorporating resilience-building practices into your daily life can help you better handle challenges and setbacks. Here are some practical tips:

1. DailyReflection: Spendafewminuteseachdayreflecting on your experiences and identifying lessons learned. This practice helps you gain perspective and recognize your growth.
2. Gratitude Journaling: Keep a gratitude journal to remind

yourself of the positive aspects of your life. Focusing on gratitude can boost your resilience by shifting your mindset to a more positive outlook.

3. Set Micro-Goals: Set small, achievable goals each day. Completing these micro-goals provides a sense of accomplishment and builds momentum.
4. Practice Mindfulness: Engage in mindfulness exercises, such as deep breathing or meditation, to manage stress and stay present. Mindfulness helps you maintain emotional balance during difficult times.

5. Stay Physically Active: Regular physical activity boosts your mood and energy levels, making it easier to handle stress and setbacks.

6. Seek Feedback: Actively seek feedback from others to gain new perspectives and identify areas for improvement. Constructive feedback helps you grow and become more resilient.
7. Help Others: Volunteering or helping others in need can provide a sense of purpose and increase your resilience. Acts of kindness and support build a strong sense of community and interconnectedness.

Building resilience is a powerful tool in overcoming procrastination. By developing our ability to bounce back from setbacks, maintain a positive outlook, and persevere in the face of challenges, we can reduce our tendency to put off important tasks.

As you move forward in your journey to overcome procrastination, embrace the opportunities for growth that come with each challenge. Remember, resilience is not about never failing or never procrastinating. It's about how we respond when we do. With practice and patience, we can strengthen our resilience muscle, making it easier to tackle tasks promptly and effectively.

Surround yourself with supportive relationships, maintain perspective, and develop effective coping strategies to navigate challenges with confidence and determination.

Are you ready to build resilience and transform your approach to overcoming failure?

> *"Hardships often prepare ordinary people for an extraordinary destiny."*
> *– C.S. Lewis*

13

Using Technology to Your Advantage: Productivity Tools

"Technology is best when it brings people together."
– Matt Mullenweg

In today's digital age, technology offers countless tools to enhance productivity and efficiency. From task management apps to collaboration platforms, these tools can help you stay organized, manage your time effectively, and achieve your goals. However, with so many options available, it can be overwhelming to choose the right tools. This chapter will explore how to leverage technology to boost productivity, providing an overview of essential tools, their benefits, and practical tips for integrating them into your daily routine.

The Role of Technology in Productivity

Technology can significantly enhance productivity by:

1. Streamlining Tasks: Automating repetitive tasks saves time and reduces human error.
2. Improving Communication: Collaboration tools facilitate seamless communication and information sharing.
3. Enhancing Organization: Digital planners and task managers help keep track of tasks, deadlines, and priorities.
4. Providing Insights: Analytics tools offer insights into your performance, helping you identify areas for improvement.
5. Boosting Motivation: Gamified productivity apps can make task completion more engaging and rewarding.

"Technology is a useful servant but a dangerous master."
- Christian Lous Lange

When used mindfully, technology can significantly enhance our efficiency and effectiveness. However, when we allow it to control our attention, it can become a major source of distraction and procrastination. The key is to approach technology with intention, selecting and using tools that genuinely support our productivity goals.

Essential Productivity Tools

To make the most of technology, it's important to choose tools that align with your needs and preferences. Here are some essential categories of productivity tools and popular options within each:

Task Management Popular Tools:

- Todoist: Aversatiletaskmanagerthatallowsyoutocreate tasks, set deadlines, and organize projects with labels and filters.
- Trello: A visual project management tool that uses boards, lists, and cards to organize tasks and track progress.
- Asana: A comprehensive project management platform that enables team collaboration, task assignment, and progress tracking.

Benefits:

- Keepstasksorganizedandprioritized.
- Providesaclearoverviewofyourworkload.
- Enhances collaboration and accountability in team settings.

Time Management Popular Tools:

- Toggl: A time tracking tool that helps you monitor how much time you spend on different tasks and projects.
- RescueTime: An app that tracks your digital activities and provides insights into how you spend your time.

- Focus@Will: A music app designed to improve focus and productivity by providing background music scientifically optimized for concentration.

Benefits:

- Helps identify time-wasting activities.
- Provides data to optimize your schedule.
- Enhances focus and reduces distractions.

Note-Taking Popular Tools:

- Evernote: A feature-rich note-taking app that allows you to capture ideas, create to-do lists, and save web clippings.
- Microsoft OneNote: A digital notebook that integrates with other Microsoft Office tools and supports multimedia notes.

- Notion: A versatile tool that combines note-taking, task management, and collaboration features.

Benefits:

- Keeps information organized and easily accessible.
- Facilitates brainstorming and idea capture.
- Enhances collaboration through shared notes and documents.

Collaboration and Communication Popular Tools:

- Slack: A messaging platform that facilitates team communication through channels, direct messages, and integra-

tions with other tools.
- Microsoft Teams: A collaboration hub that combines chat, video conferencing, file sharing, and integration with Microsoft Office.
- Zoom: A video conferencing tool that supports virtual meetings, webinars, and collaboration features like screen sharing and breakout rooms.

Benefits:

- Enhances team communication and collaboration.
- Reduces the need for in-person meetings.
- Supports remote work and virtual collaboration.

File Storage and Sharing Popular Tools:

- Google Drive: A cloud storage service that allows you to store, share, and collaborate on files and documents.
- Dropbox: A file hosting service that offers cloud storage, file synchronization, and personal cloud.
- OneDrive: Microsoft's cloud storage service that integrates with Microsoft Office and supports file sharing and collaboration.

Benefits:

- Provides secure, accessible storage for files and documents.
- Facilitates file sharing and collaboration.
- Supports remote access and backup of important data.

Mark, a freelance graphic designer, found himself struggling with procrastination and missed deadlines. He decided to implement a productivity system using technology.

He started by using Trello to manage his projects, breaking them down into smaller, manageable tasks. For time tracking, he implemented Toggl, which helped him understand how he was spending his work hours and identify time-wasting activities.

To combat distractions, Mark used the Freedom app to block social media sites during his designated work hours. He also started using the Pomodoro technique with the help of the Focus To-Do app, which helped him maintain focus for shorter periods and take regular breaks.

For note-taking and brainstorming, Mark chose Evernote, which allowed him to jot down ideas whenever inspiration struck and access them from all his devices.

Initially, juggling all these new tools felt overwhelming. But Mark started slowly, introducing one tool at a time and giving himself time to adjust. He also took advantage of the integration features between some of these apps to create a more seamless workflow.

After a few months, Mark noticed a significant improvement in his productivity. He was meeting deadlines more consistently, felt less stressed about his workload, and even had time to take on additional projects. The key to his success was not just the tools themselves, but his consistent and intentional use of them.

Overcoming Common Challenges

While productivity tools can be incredibly helpful, they come with their own set of challenges. Here's how to address some common issues:

Tool Overload
It's easy to fall into the trap of using too many tools, which can itself become a form of procrastination.
Solution: Regularly audit your tools. If you haven't used a tool in the last month, consider removing it from your workflow.

Learning Curve
Some productivity tools have steep learning curves, which can be discouraging.
Solution: Give yourself time to learn. Many tools offer tutorials or have active user communities where you can seek help.

Over-Reliance on Tools
Becoming too dependent on tools can lead to a false sense of productivity.
Solution: Remember that tools are meant to support your productivity, not replace your own effort and decision-making.

Syncing and Technical Issues
Technical problems can be frustrating and lead to procrasti-

nation.

Solution: Have a backup system in place. For crucial tasks, consider having a low-tech alternative (like a physical notebook) as a backup.

Privacy Concerns

Some people hesitate to use productivity tools due to data privacy concerns.

Solution: Research the privacy policies of the tools you're considering. Many offer robust privacy settings that you can customize.

Integrating Productivity Tools into Your Routine

Choosing the right tools is just the first step; effectively integrating them into your daily routine is crucial for maximizing their benefits. Here are some tips for making the most of productivity tools:

1. Start with a Few Tools: Begin with a few essential tools and gradually incorporate more as needed. Overloading yourself with too many tools at once can be counterproductive.

2. Customize Your Setup: Personalize the tools to suit your workflow. For example, create custom task labels in Todoist or organize Trello boards according to your project stages.

3. Set Clear Goals: Use productivity tools to set specific, measurable goals. For instance, use Toggl to track time spent on a particular project and aim to reduce time

wastage.

4. Establish Routines: Create daily and weekly routines that incorporate your productivity tools. For example, start each day by reviewing your tasks in Asana and end with a quick review of completed tasks.

5. Leverage Integrations: Many productivity tools offer integrations with other apps. Use these integrations to streamline your workflow and avoid switching between multiple platforms.

6. Monitor and Adjust: Regularly review your productivity data and adjust your approach as needed. Use insights from tools like RescueTime to identify areas for improve- ment.

7. Stay Consistent: Consistency is key to building productive habits. Make it a habit to use your chosen tools regularly and integrate them into your routine.

Let us see some scenarios of Technology Boosting Productivity in real life.

Jessica, a freelance writer, uses a combination of Todoist for task management, Toggl for time tracking, and Google Drive for file storage. By organizing her tasks in Todoist, she ensures that she meets deadlines. Toggl helps her track how much time she spends on each project, allowing her to optimize her schedule and manage her workload effectively. Storing her files in Google Drive ensures that she can access her work from anywhere and collaborate with clients seamlessly.

The team at a small marketing agency uses Slack for commu- nication, Trello for project management, and Zoom for virtual meetings. Slack channels keep their discussions organized by topic, Trello boards help them track project progress, and Zoom meetings facilitate remote collaboration. This integrated setup enhances their communication, keeps everyone aligned, and ensures that projects stay on track.

Alex, a college student, uses Notion for note-taking, Microsoft OneDrive for file storage, and Focus@Will for concentration. Notion helps Alex keep all his class notes and assignments organized in one place, OneDrive ensures that his files are securely stored and accessible from any device, and Focus@Will's music helps him stay focused during study sessions. This combination of tools enhances his productivity and academic performance.

> *"Productivity is never an accident. It is always the result of a commitment to excellence, intelligent planning, and focused effort."*
> *– Paul J. Meyer*

Technology, when used mindfully, can be a powerful ally in overcoming procrastination and boosting productivity. The key is to approach these tools with intention, selecting those that genuinely address your specific productivity challenges and integrating them thoughtfully into your workflow.

Remember, productivity tools are just that - tools. They're meant to support and enhance your efforts, not to magically solve all your productivity issues. The most important factor is still your commitment to overcoming procrastination and becoming more productive.

As you explore different productivity tools, be patient with yourself. It may take some trial and error to find the combination that works best for you. Don't be afraid to experiment with different tools and approaches until you find your ideal productivity system.

By harnessing the power of technology in your fight against procrastination, you're equipping yourself with valuable allies. Used wisely, these tools can help you stay organized, focused, and motivated, turning your productivity aspirations into reality.

Are you ready to leverage technology to boost your productivity and achieve your goals?

14

Creating a Morning Routine: Start Your Day Right

"The early morning has gold in its mouth." – Benjamin Franklin

How you start your morning sets the tone for the rest of your day. A well-planned morning routine can be a powerful tool in combating procrastination, significantly boost your productivity, improve your mood, and help you achieve your daily goals. This chapter explores the importance of a morning routine, how to create one that suits your lifestyle, and practical tips for maintaining it. By the end of this chapter, you'll have a blueprint for starting your day right and maximizing your productivity.

"Win the morning, win the day." - Tim Ferriss

This quote from productivity expert Tim Ferriss encapsulates the importance of a strong morning routine. By starting your day with intention and purpose, you set yourself up for success and reduce the likelihood of falling into procrastination traps later in the day.

The Importance of a Morning Routine

A morning routine is more than just a series of activities; it's a foundation for a successful day. Here's why a morning routine is crucial:

1. SetsaPositiveTone: Aconsistentroutinehelpsyoustart your day with intention and focus.
2. Enhances Productivity: Structured mornings can lead to increased efficiency and better time management throughout the day.
3. Reduces Stress: Knowing what to expect in the morning can reduce anxiety and help you feel more in control.
4. Improves Health: Incorporating healthy habits like exercise and a nutritious breakfast can boost your physical and mental well-being.
5. Builds Momentum: Completing morning tasks creates a sense of accomplishment that motivates you to tackle more throughout the day.

Sample Morning Routine
Here's a sample morning routine to inspire you:

- 6:00AM:Wakeupanddrinkaglassofwater.
- 6:10AM:Exercisefor30minutes(jogging,yoga,orahome

workout).
- 6:40 AM: Shower and get ready for the day.
- 7:00 AM: Eat a healthy breakfast (e.g., oatmeal with fruits and nuts, a smoothie, or scrambled eggs with vegetables).
- 7:30 AM: Spend 10 minutes journaling or meditating.
- 7:45 AM: Review your to-do list and plan your day.
- 8:00 AM: Start your first task of the day.

Elements of an Effective Morning Routine

While everyone's ideal morning routine will be different, there are some common elements that many successful people incorporate:

Wake Up Early and Consistently
  Set a consistent wake-up time, even on weekends. This helps regulate your body's internal clock.

Hydrate
  Drink a glass of water first thing in the morning to rehydrate after sleep.

Move Your Body
  Engage in some form of physical activity, whether it's a full workout, yoga, or a quick stretch.

Mindfulness Practice
  Incorporate meditation, deep breathing, or journaling to center your mind.

Nutritious Breakfast

Fuel your body and brain with a healthy breakfast.

Plan Your Day
Review your goals and priorities for the day ahead.

Personal Growth
Spend some time reading, listening to a podcast, or learning something new.

Tackle an Important Task
Use your morning energy to complete a significant task.

William used to start his days rushing and stressed. He'd hit snooze multiple times, scroll through social media in bed, then hurry to get ready, often skipping breakfast. He frequently arrived at work feeling frazzled and unprepared, leading to procrastination on important tasks.

Determined to change, William created a new morning routine:
 6:00 AM: Wake up consistently (even on weekends)
 6:05 AM: Drink a glass of water and do 5 minutes of stretching
 6:15 AM: 10-minute meditation using a guided app
 6:30 AM: 20-minute jog around the neighborhood
 7:00 AM: Shower and get ready
 7:30 AM: Eat a nutritious breakfast while reviewing his daily goals
 8:00 AM: Leave for work

After sticking to this routine for a month, William noticed significant changes. He arrived at work feeling energized, focused, and prepared. His tendency to procrastinate decreased, and he found himself tackling important tasks earlier in the day when his energy was highest.

> *"We are what we repeatedly do. Excellence, then, is not an act, but a habit."*
> *- Aristotle*

This quote reminds us that creating a successful morning routine is about building positive habits over time.

Overcoming Common Challenges

Creating and sticking to a morning routine can come with its own set of challenges. Here's how to address some common ones:

Difficulty Waking Up Early
Solution: Gradually adjust your wake-up time in 15-minute increments. Ensure you're getting enough sleep by going to bed earlier.

Lack of Motivation
Solution: Start with activities you enjoy. As you begin to feel the benefits of your routine, this will provide motivation to continue.

Inconsistency
   Solution: Use habit-stacking (linking a new habit to an existing one) to make your routine more automatic. For example,

"After I brush my teeth, I will meditate for 5 minutes."

Feeling Rushed
   Solution: Wake up a bit earlier or streamline your routine. Remember, quality is more important than quantity.

Family Responsibilities
Solution: Involve your family in parts of your routine or adjust your wake-up time to have some quiet time before family obligations begin.

> *"How you start your day is how you live your day. How you live your day is how you live your life."*
> *- Louise Hay*

Tips for Maintaining Your Morning Routine

Creating a routine is just the first step; maintaining it consistently can be challenging. Here are some tips to help you stick to your morning routine:

1. Start Small: Begin with a few activities and gradually add more as you become comfortable.
2. Be Flexible: Allow for adjustments on days when things don't go as planned. Flexibility helps you stay committed without feeling overwhelmed.
3. Prepare the Night Before: Set out your workout clothes, plan your breakfast, and review your schedule the night before to streamline your morning.
4. Track Your Progress: Use a journal or an app to track your morning routine and note any benefits or challenges.

5. Stay Motivated: Remind yourself of the benefits of a morning routine and how it positively impacts your day.

Tim Cook, CEO of Apple, starts his day at 4:00 AM to tackle emails and get a head start on the day. He then heads to the gym for a workout, ensuring he begins his day with physical activity and mental clarity.

Oprah Winfrey begins her day with meditation, followed by exercise. She then enjoys a healthy breakfast and spends time reading and planning her day. This balanced routine helps her maintain focus and well-being.

Benjamin Franklin had a structured morning routine that included waking up early, addressing personal goals, planning his day, and taking time for reflection. His disciplined approach contributed to his productivity and success.

> "Your morning routine generates a 10x return for good or for bad. Make it good."
> – Todd Stocker

Creating a morning routine is not about adhering to a rigid set of rules or forcing yourself into a one-size-fits-all program. It's about intentionally designing the start of your day in a way that sets you up for success and reduces the likelihood of procrastination.

The perfect morning routine is the one that works for you. It should leave you feeling energized, focused, and ready to tackle your day. Don't be afraid to experiment with different activities and timings until you find what fits best with your lifestyle and goals.

By starting your day with intention and purpose, you create a strong foundation for productivity. This proactive approach can significantly reduce your tendency to procrastinate, as you'll begin each day with clarity, energy, and momentum.

Even if you don't stick to your routine perfectly every day, the effort to start your day mindfully will still yield benefits. Over time, as your morning routine becomes a habit, you'll likely find that procrastination becomes less of a struggle and productivity becomes more natural.

Your morning routine is your secret weapon against procrastination. Use it wisely, adjust it as needed, and watch as it transforms not just your mornings, but your entire approach to productivity and goal achievement.

Are you ready to create a morning routine that sets you up for success?

> *"An early-morning walk is a blessing for the whole day." – Henry David Thoreau*

15

Avoiding Multitasking: Focus on One Thing

"Multitasking is a lie."
- Gary Keller, author of "The ONE Thing"

In our fast-paced world, multitasking is often seen as a valuable skill. However, when it comes to productivity and overcoming procrastination, focusing on one thing at a time is far more effective. This chapter will explore why multitasking is counterproductive and how to cultivate the ability to focus on a single task.

The Myth of Multitasking

Many people believe that multitasking helps them get more done in less time. However, this is a myth. Here's why multitasking is counterproductive:

1. Reduced Efficiency: Switching between tasks often leads to a loss of focus and efficiency. The brain requires time to reorient itself each time you switch tasks, leading to wasted time and mental energy.
2. Increased Errors: Multitasking increases the likelihood of making mistakes. When your attention is divided, you're more prone to errors in each task.
3. Mental Fatigue: Constantly switching tasks can exhaust your brain, leading to quicker burnout and reduced overall performance.
4. Shallow Work: Multitasking often leads to shallow work, where tasks are completed superficially without deep thought or quality.

"Multitasking is the ability to screw everything up simultaneously."
– Jeremy Clarkson

Benefits of Focusing on One Task

Focusing on one task at a time, also known as single-tasking, can lead to significant improvements in productivity and quality of work. Here are some benefits of single-tasking:

1. Enhanced Concentration: Focusing on one task allows for deeper concentration and immersion, leading to higher-quality work.
2. Better Quality: With your full attention on one task, you're more likely to produce better, more accurate results.
3. Increased Productivity: Single-tasking can actually make

you more productive by reducing the time wasted on task-switching.

4. Reduced Stress: Focusing on one task at a time can lower stress levels, as you're not constantly juggling multiple demands.

5. Improved Creativity: Deep focus on a single task can lead to greater insights and creative solutions.

> *"The ability to focus on a single task for an extended period is essential to achieving mastery."*
> *– Cal Newport*

Jack prided himself on his ability to "multitask." On a typical day, he would have multiple browser tabs open, respond to emails while on conference calls, and work on several projects simultaneously. Despite feeling busy, Jack often ended his days feeling like he hadn't accomplished much. He frequently procrastinated on important tasks, feeling overwhelmed by his workload.

After learning about the downsides of multitasking, Jack decided to change his approach. He began dedicating focused time to individual tasks, closing unnecessary browser tabs, and turning off notifications during work sessions. Initially, this felt uncomfortable and less productive. However, after a few weeks, Jack noticed he was completing tasks more quickly and with fewer errors. His sense of overwhelm decreased, and he found himself procrastinating less on important projects.

> *"Concentrate all your thoughts upon the work at hand. The sun's rays do not burn until brought to a focus."*

- Alexander Graham Bell

Strategies to Avoid Multitasking and Focus on One Thing

Transitioning from multitasking to single-tasking requires deliberate effort and strategies. Here are some practical tips to help you focus on one thing at a time:

Prioritize Your Tasks

- Use tools like the Eisenhower Matrix to prioritize tasks based on their urgency and importance. Focus on high-priority tasks first.

Time Blocking

- Allocate specific blocks of time for different tasks throughout your day. During these blocks, focus solely on the designated task and avoid interruptions.

Set Clear Goals

- Define clear, specific goals for each task. Having a clear objective helps you stay focused and motivated.

Eliminate Distractions

- Identifyandminimizedistractionsinyourenvironment. This might include turning off notifications, creating a dedicated workspace, and setting boundaries with colleagues or family.

Practice Mindfulness

- Mindfulness exercises can help improve your ability to focus. Practices like meditation and deep breathing can train your brain to stay present and attentive.

Use the Pomodoro Technique

- The Pomodoro Technique involves working for a set period (e.g., 25 minutes) followed by a short break. This method helps maintain focus while providing regular intervals for rest.

Break Tasks into Smaller Steps

- Breaking tasks into smaller, manageable steps can make them less overwhelming and easier to tackle one at a time.

Set Boundaries

- Communicate your need for uninterrupted work time to colleagues, friends, and family. Setting boundaries helps create a focused work environment.

Overcoming Common Challenges

Transitioning from multitasking to single-tasking can be challenging. Here are some common obstacles and how to overcome them:

Fear of Missing Out (FOMO)
Challenge: Worry about missing important messages or updates.
Solution: Set specific times to check emails and messages. Communicate your availability to colleagues.

Difficulty Concentrating
Challenge: Struggling to maintain focus on one task.
Solution: Start with shorter focus periods (e.g., 10 minutes) and gradually increase. Practice mindfulness to improve concentration.

Pressure to Multitask
Challenge: Workplace expectations of constant availability.
Solution: Communicate the benefits of focused work to your team. Lead by example and share productivity gains.

Habit of Task-Switching
Challenge: Ingrained habit of jumping between tasks.
Solution: Use visual cues (like a "Do Not Disturb" sign) to remind yourself to stay focused. Track how often you switch tasks to increase awareness.

Feelings of Reduced Productivity
Challenge: Single-tasking might initially feel less productive.
Solution: Track your actual output and quality of work to see the real benefits. Be patient as you adjust to the new approach.

> *"The man who chases two rabbits catches neither."*
> *- Confucius*

Sarah, a marketing professional, used to juggle multiple projects at once, leading to frequent mistakes and burnout. By adopting single-tasking strategies like time blocking and eliminating distractions, she noticed a significant improvement in her productivity and the quality of her work.

Bill Gates is known for his "Think Weeks," where he isolates himself for a week to focus solely on reading and deep thinking. This dedicated time for single-tasking has been instrumental in his innovative ideas and strategic planning.

While writing the "Harry Potter" series, J.K. Rowling would often seclude herself in a hotel room to focus entirely on her writing, free from distractions. This intense focus allowed her to create one of the most successful book series of all time.

Steve Jobs was known for his ability to focus intensely on one thing at a time. He would often simplify his priorities to ensure he could dedicate his full attention to what mattered most, leading to groundbreaking innovations at Apple.

> *"You can do two things at once, but you can't focus effectively on two things at once."*
> *– Gary Keller*

Avoiding multitasking and focusing on one task at a time is a powerful strategy to enhance productivity, reduce stress, and improve the quality of your work. By prioritizing tasks, eliminating distractions, and practicing mindfulness, you can develop the habit of single-tasking and achieve greater success in your personal and professional life. Embrace the benefits of focused work and take control of your productivity today.

As you cultivate this skill, you may find that tasks you once procrastinated on become more manageable. The overwhelm that often leads to procrastination can diminish when we approach our work one focused step at a time.

Be patient with yourself as you make this transition. Like any skill, single-tasking takes practice. Celebrate your progress, no matter how small, and keep in mind the long-term benefits of this approach.

> *"The successful warrior is the average man, with laser-like focus."*
> *- Bruce Lee*

Let this quote inspire you to cultivate your focus. With practice and persistence, you can develop the "laser-like focus" that Bruce Lee speaks of, becoming more productive and less prone to procrastination.

Are you ready to break free from the myth of multitasking and focus on what truly matters?

16

Taking Breaks: Rest and Recharge

"Take rest; a field that has rested gives a bountiful crop."
– Ovid

In our fast-paced world, it can be tempting to work non-stop to get everything done. However, taking regular breaks is crucial for maintaining productivity, creativity, and overall well-being. This chapter will explore the importance of taking breaks, different types of breaks, and strategies to rest and recharge effectively. By the end of this chapter, you'll understand how to incorporate breaks into your routine to boost your performance and prevent burnout.

"Almost everything will work again if you unplug it for a few minutes, including you."
– Anne Lamott

This humorous quote captures a fundamental truth about human productivity. Like our electronic devices, our brains need regular "unplugging" to function at their best.

The Importance of Taking Breaks

Taking breaks might seem counterintuitive to productivity, but they are essential for several reasons:

1. Improves Focus: Breaks help prevent mental fatigue and keep your attention sharp.
2. BoostsCreativity: Steppingawayfromataskcanprovide new perspectives and foster creative thinking.
3. Reduces Stress: Short breaks can lower stress levels and prevent burnout.
4. Enhances Learning and Memory: Breaks give your brain time to consolidate information, improving learning and memory retention.
5. Increases Productivity: Regular breaks can prevent the decline in performance that often accompanies long periods of continuous work.

Types of Breaks

Not all breaks are created equal. Here are some effective types of breaks to consider:

Microbreaks (30 seconds to 5 minutes)
 - Stretch or do quick exercises
 - Practice deep breathing

- Look away from your screen and focus on a distant object

Short Breaks (5 to 15 minutes)
   - Take a short walk
   - Have a healthy snack
   - Do a quick meditation session

Longer Breaks (15 to 60 minutes)
   - Eat a proper meal
   - Exercise
   - Engage in a hobby or relaxing activity

Extended Breaks (hours to days)
   - Weekends off
   - Vacations
   - Sabbaticals

Rachel often found herself procrastinating on challenging projects. She would sit at her desk for hours, feeling guilty about taking breaks, but her productivity would steadily decline.

After learning about the importance of breaks, Rachel implemented a new routine:
   - She used the Pomodoro Technique, working in 25-minute focused sessions followed by 5-minute breaks.
   - During her short breaks, she would stretch, do some deep breathing, or step outside for fresh air.
   - Every 2-3 hours, she took a longer 15-30 minute break to go for a walk or practice a quick meditation.

Initially, Rachel felt anxious about "wasting time" on breaks. However, she soon noticed that she was more focused during her work sessions and less likely to procrastinate. Her creativity improved, and she found solutions to design problems more easily. Most importantly, her overall enjoyment of her work increased, further reducing her tendency to procrastinate.

Strategies for Effective Breaks

Schedule Your Breaks
   Don't leave breaks to chance. Plan them into your day just as you would any other important task.

Set Clear Start and End Times
   Having defined break periods helps you fully relax during the break and refocus when it's time to return to work.

Step Away from Your Workspace
   Physically removing yourself from your work environment, even if just for a few minutes, can provide mental distance and refresh your perspective.

Engage in Activities You Enjoy
Use break time for activities that you find genuinely relaxing or energizing. This makes breaks something to look forward to rather than another task.

Practice Mindfulness
Use breaks as an opportunity to practice mindfulness. This can help clear your mind and improve focus when you return

to work.

Hydrate and Nourish
Use break times to drink water and have healthy snacks. Proper hydration and nutrition are crucial for maintaining energy and focus.

Move Your Body
Incorporate physical movement into your breaks. Even short periods of activity can boost energy and mood.

> *"The time to relax is when you don't have time for it."* -
> *Sydney J. Harris*

Overcoming Guilt and Resistance to Taking Breaks

Many people struggle with feeling guilty about taking breaks. Here's how to overcome this:

Reframe Your Thinking
View breaks as a productivity tool rather than a sign of laziness. Remind yourself that breaks enhance your overall effectiveness.

Start Small
If taking regular breaks feels challenging, start with short, 5-minute breaks and gradually increase their duration.

Track Your Productivity
Monitor your productivity levels with and without regular breaks. Seeing the positive impact can help alleviate guilt.

Communicate with Others
If you're worried about how breaks might be perceived by colleagues or supervisors, communicate the productivity benefits of your break strategy.

Create a Break-Friendly Culture
If you're in a leadership position, encourage a workplace culture that values regular breaks and recharging.

Tom, a software engineer, prided himself on his ability to work long hours without breaks. He often procrastinated on difficult coding problems, feeling overwhelmed but guilty about stepping away.

After experiencing burnout, Tom decided to change his approach:
- He set alarms on his phone to remind him to take short breaks every hour.
- During these breaks, he would step away from his computer and do some quick stretches or take a brief walk.
- He started taking a proper lunch break away from his desk, using this time to eat mindfully and relax.
- On weekends, he made a point of fully disconnecting from work.

Initially, Tom felt anxious about falling behind. However, he soon noticed that he was solving complex coding problems more efficiently and procrastinating less on challenging tasks. His overall job satisfaction improved, and he found himself more energized and creative in his work.

Leveraging Breaks to Combat Specific Types of Procrastination

Different types of breaks can be particularly effective for specific procrastination challenges:

For Decision Paralysis
  - Take a short walk to clear your mind
  - Use a break for quick meditation to reduce anxiety

For Perfectionism-Induced Procrastination
  - Use breaks to remind yourself of the big picture
  - Practice self-compassion exercises during break times

For Overwhelm-Related Procrastination
  - Use breaks to break down large tasks into smaller, manageable steps
  - Practice gratitude during breaks to shift perspective

For Boredom-Induced Procrastination
  - Use breaks for activities that spark joy and reignite motivation
  - Learn something new during longer breaks to stimulate your mind

For Fear-Based Procrastination
  - Use breaks for positive visualization exercises
  - Practice deep breathing or progressive muscle relaxation during breaks

The Role of Extended Breaks
While daily breaks are crucial, extended periods of rest are equally important:

Weekends
Take full weekends off when possible. Use this time to completely disconnect from work, engage in hobbies, and spend time with loved ones.

Vacations
Regular vacations are essential for long-term productivity and preventing burnout. Fully disconnect during these times to allow for deep recharging.

Sabbaticals
If possible, consider taking extended periods off work. Sabbaticals can provide profound rest and often lead to increased creativity and motivation upon return.

Thomas Edison was known for taking short naps throughout the day to recharge. His ability to rest and rejuvenate allowed him to work long hours and maintain high productivity levels.

Winston Churchill famously took daily naps during World War II. These naps helped him maintain the stamina needed for his demanding role as Prime Minister.

Arianna Huffington, founder of the Huffington Post, advocates for the importance of sleep and breaks. After experiencing burnout, she implemented breaks and naps into her routine, leading to improved productivity and well-being.

> *"Sometimes the most productive thing you can do is relax."*
> *– Mark Black*

As you move forward in your journey to overcome procrastination, make regular breaks a non-negotiable part of your routine. Start small if needed, but be consistent. Pay attention to how different types of breaks affect your energy, focus, and motivation.

> *"There is virtue in work and there is virtue in rest. Use both and overlook neither."*
> *- Alan Cohen*

Let this quote inspire you to find the right balance between focused work and rejuvenating rest. By mastering this balance, you'll be well-equipped to overcome procrastination, boost your productivity, and achieve your goals while maintaining your well-being.

Taking breaks is essential for maintaining productivity, creativity, and well-being. By understanding the importance of breaks, incorporating different types of breaks into your routine, and adopting effective strategies, you can rest and recharge effectively. Overcoming challenges to taking breaks requires intention and planning, but the benefits are well worth the effort. Embrace the power of breaks and make them an integral part of your daily routine to achieve greater success and well-being.

Are you ready to take a break and recharge?

17

Seeking Help When Needed: Don't Be Afraid to Ask

"Asking for help isn't a sign of weakness, it's a sign of strength."
– Barack Obama

Procrastination often feels like a solitary battle, a personal struggle against our own minds. However, one of the most powerful tools in overcoming this challenge is something many of us overlook: seeking help. This chapter delves into the importance of reaching out for assistance, the barriers that may hold us back, and strategies for effectively seeking and utilizing help in our journey to conquer procrastination.

The Importance of Asking for Help
Seeking help when needed is crucial for several reasons:

1. Overcoming Obstacles: Assistance from others can help you overcome challenges and roadblocks more quickly.
2. Gaining New Perspectives: Others can offer fresh perspectives and insights that you might not have consid- ered.
3. ImprovingEfficiency: Delegatingtasksorseekingexpertise can lead to more efficient and effective outcomes.
4. LearningandGrowth: Collaboratingwithothersprovides opportunities for learning and personal growth.
5. Building Relationships: Asking for help fosters collaboration and strengthens relationships within your personal and professional networks.

Recognizing When You Need Help
Before we can ask for help, we need to recognize when we need it. This self-awareness is crucial but often challenging, especially when we're deep in the throes of procrastination. Here are some signs that indicate you might benefit from seeking assistance:

a) Persistent Procrastination: If you find yourself consistently putting off tasks, despite your best intentions and efforts to change, it may be time to seek help.
b) Negative Impact on Life: When procrastination starts affecting your work performance, relationships, or overall well-being, it's a clear sign that you need support.
c) Overwhelming Feelings: If you frequently feel over-

whelmed by your to-do list or the mere thought of starting tasks induces anxiety, reaching out for help could provide relief.

d) Lack of Progress: If you've tried various techniques to combat procrastination but haven't seen significant improvement, external input could be valuable.

e) Isolation: Feeling alone in your struggle or avoiding social interactions due to unfinished tasks is a red flag that shouldn't be ignored.

Remember, recognizing the need for help is not a sign of weakness but a demonstration of self-awareness and a commitment to personal growth. As psychologist Margie Warrell puts it, "Courage is not the absence of fear, but the willingness to act in its presence." Acknowledging that you need help takes courage, and it's the first step towards positive change.

Overcoming the Fear of Asking for Help

Despite knowing that we need help, many of us still hesitate to ask for it. This reluctance often stems from various fears and misconceptions. Let's explore some common barriers and how to overcome them.

Fear of Appearing Incompetent:
Many people worry that asking for help will make them look weak or incapable. However, research suggests the opposite. A study by Harvard Business School found that individuals who seek advice are perceived as more competent, not less.

Brené Brown, a research professor and author, emphasizes the power of vulnerability: "Vulnerability is not winning or losing; it's having the courage to show up and be seen when we have no control over the outcome." By asking for help, you're demonstrating self-awareness and a commitment to growth – qualities that are highly respected.

Strategy to overcome: Reframe asking for help as a strength. Remind yourself that seeking assistance shows you're proactive and committed to improvement.

Worry About Burdening Others:
We often hesitate to ask for help because we don't want to impose on others. However, research in social psychology has shown that people generally underestimate others' willingness to help. In fact, many people feel good about being asked for help, as it makes them feel trusted and valued.

Strategy to overcome: Remember that most people are willing to help if asked. Be specific about what you need and respectful of their time. Offer to reciprocate in the future.

Pride or Stubbornness:
Sometimes, our own ego gets in the way of seeking help. We might feel that we should be able to handle everything on our own. However, this mindset can be counterproductive and lead to increased stress and decreased performance.

As the ancient proverb goes, "He who asks a question remains a fool for five minutes. He who does not ask remains a fool forever."

Strategy to overcome: Practice humility. Recognize that everyone needs help sometimes, and that being able to ask for it is a sign of emotional intelligence and maturity.

Past Negative Experiences:

If you've had unhelpful or dismissive responses when asking for help in the past, you might be hesitant to try again. However, it's important not to let these experiences prevent you from seeking the support you need.

Strategy to overcome: Reflect on what went wrong in past situations. Was it the person you asked, the way you asked, or the timing? Use these insights to approach help-seeking more effectively in the future.

Identifying Sources of Help

Help can come from various sources, depending on your specific needs and situation. Here are some potential sources to consider:

Friends and Family:
Your close circle can offer emotional support, accountability, or practical assistance. They know you well and can provide personalized encouragement. For instance, you might ask a friend to check in on your progress regularly or to work alongside you during designated focus times.

Colleagues or Classmates:
These individuals can be particularly helpful for work or study-related procrastination issues. They understand the context of your tasks and might have faced similar challenges. You could form a study group or set up regular check-ins with a coworker to discuss progress and challenges.

Mentors or Supervisors:
More experienced individuals in your field can offer valuable

guidance and help you develop better time management skills. They might share strategies that have worked for them or provide a broader perspective on prioritizing tasks.

Professional Help:
Therapists, counselors, or coaches specializing in procrastination can provide targeted strategies and support. They can help you uncover underlying causes of your procrastination and develop personalized techniques to overcome it.

Online Communities:
Forums, social media groups, or specialized platforms dedicated to productivity and overcoming procrastination can be valuable resources. These communities allow you to connect with others facing similar challenges, share experiences, and learn new strategies.

Books and Courses:
While not direct human help, self-help books, online courses, or workshops on procrastination and time management can provide structured guidance and tools.

How to Ask for Help Effectively

Once you've identified potential sources of help, the next step is to actually ask for it. Here are some strategies to make your request for help more effective:

Be Specific:
Clearly articulate what kind of help you need. Instead of saying, "I'm struggling with procrastination," try something

like, "Could you check in with me daily about my progress on the project?" or "I need help breaking down this large task into manageable steps."

Choose the Right Time and Place:
Pick a moment when the person you're asking isn't rushed or distracted. If it's a significant request, consider scheduling a specific time to discuss it.

Explain the Situation:
Provide context for your request. Briefly explain your struggle with procrastination and why you're seeking help. This helps the person understand the importance of your request.

Show Appreciation:
Express gratitude for any help offered, even if it's not exactly what you were hoping for. Gratitude can strengthen relationships and make people more likely to help in the future.

Offer Reciprocity:
Let the person know you're willing to help them in return if they ever need it. This creates a mutually beneficial relationship.

Be Open to Suggestions:
The person you're asking might have ideas you haven't considered. Be open to their suggestions, even if they're different from what you initially had in mind.

Follow Up:
After receiving help, keep the person updated on your

progress. This shows that you value their assistance and are putting it to good use.

Making the Most of Help Received

Receiving help is just the first step. To truly benefit from it, you need to utilize the assistance effectively:

Implement Advice:
Take action on the suggestions or strategies provided. As author Stephen King notes, "The scariest moment is always just before you start. After that, things can only get better." This applies not just to tasks you've been procrastinating on, but also to implementing new anti-procrastination strategies.

Reflect and Adapt:
Regularly reflect on the effectiveness of the help you're receiving. What's working well? What might need adjustment? Use these insights to refine your approach.

Communicate Openly:
If something isn't working, communicate this clearly with the person helping you. They might have alternative suggestions or be able to modify their approach.

Practice Self-Compassion:
Remember that overcoming procrastination is a process. Be kind to yourself if you experience setbacks, and use them as learning opportunities.

Pay It Forward:

As you make progress, consider sharing your experiences and insights with others who are struggling with procrastination. Teaching others can reinforce your own learning and provide a sense of purpose.

Building a Support Network

Over time, aim to build a network of support that you can rely on:

Diversify Your Support:
Different people can help in different ways. Some might be great for emotional support, while others might excel at practical problem-solving. Build a diverse network to cover various needs.

Join Support Groups:
Look for local or online groups focused on overcoming procrastination or improving productivity. Regular interaction with others facing similar challenges can be incredibly motivating.

Find an Accountability Partner:
Partner with someone who has similar goals. Set up regular check-ins to discuss progress, challenges, and strategies. This mutual accountability can be a powerful motivator.

Cultivate Inspiring Relationships:
Surround yourself with people who motivate and inspire you. Their energy and positive influence can be contagious.

Engage in Continuous Learning:

Attend workshops, webinars, or conferences related to productivity and personal development. These events can provide new strategies and connect you with like-minded individuals.

Use Technology:

Explore apps and online tools designed to facilitate accountability and support. Some apps allow you to connect with accountability partners or join virtual co-working sessions.

> *"You don't have to do it all by yourself. Let others help you."*
> *– Unknown*

Steve Jobs was known for surrounding himself with talented individuals and seeking their input. By asking for help and collaborating with experts, he was able to create innovative products and lead Apple to success.

Sheryl Sandberg, COO of Facebook, emphasizes the importance of asking for help in her book "Lean In." She shares how seeking mentorship and support has been crucial in her career advancement.

Richard Branson, founder of the Virgin Group, often credits his success to the people he surrounds himself with. He believes in seeking help and collaborating with others to achieve goals.

> *"The strongest people make time to help others, even if they're struggling with their own personal demons."*
> *– Unknown*

SEEKING HELP WHEN NEEDED: DON'T BE AFRAID TO ASK

Seeking help is not a sign of weakness, but a powerful strategy in overcoming procrastination. By recognizing when you need assistance, overcoming fears about asking, identifying sources of support, and using help effectively, you can make significant strides in managing procrastination.

Remember the words of motivational speaker Les Brown: "Ask for help not because you're weak, but because you want to remain strong." Your journey to overcome procrastination doesn't have to be a solitary one. Reach out, connect with others, and let their support propel you towards your goals.

As you move forward, challenge yourself to take one small step towards seeking help this week. It could be as simple as sharing your struggle with a friend or researching local support groups. Remember, every journey begins with a single step, and asking for help might just be the step that transforms your relationship with procrastination.

Are you ready to ask for the help you need to achieve your goals?

18

Staying Motivated: Find Your Why

"He who has a why to live can bear almost any how."
– Friedrich Nietzsche

Motivation is the driving force behind taking action and achieving your goals. However, staying motivated can be challenging, especially when faced with obstacles or long-term projects. This chapter will explore the importance of finding your "why," understanding what motivates you, and providing strategies to maintain and boost your motivation. By discovering your deeper purpose and learning how to stay motivated, you can sustain your efforts and achieve your goals more effectively.

The Importance of Finding Your Why

Your "why" is your underlying purpose or reason for pursuing a goal. It provides meaning and direction, making it easier to stay motivated and committed. Understanding your why is crucial for several reasons:

1. Provides Clarity: Knowing your why helps clarify your goals and priorities.
2. Increases Commitment: A strong why enhances your dedication and perseverance.
3. Boosts Resilience: Your why can help you overcome setbacks and stay focused during challenging times.
4. Enhances Fulfillment: Pursuing goals aligned with your why brings greater satisfaction and fulfillment.

Consider the story of Viktor Frankl, a psychiatrist who survived Nazi concentration camps. In his book "Man's Search for Meaning," he describes how having a strong sense of purpose - his "why" - helped him endure unimaginable hardships. For Frankl, it was the desire to reunite with his wife and rewrite his manuscript that had been destroyed.

While our challenges may be less extreme, the principle remains the same: a powerful "why" can help us overcome procrastination and stay committed to our goals.

Types of Motivation:

a) Extrinsic Motivation: This comes from external factors such as rewards, praise, or avoiding punishment. While effective in the short term, it often lacks sustaining power.

b) Intrinsic Motivation: This stems from internal desires and personal satisfaction. It's more powerful and long-lasting than extrinsic motivation.

As psychologist Edward Deci puts it, "When people are intrinsically motivated, they act for the fun or challenge entailed rather than because of external prods, pressures, or rewards."

Discovering Your Why

Finding your why involves self-reflection and understanding what truly matters to you. Here are some steps to help you discover your why:

Reflect on Your Passions and Interests

- Think about what activities, topics, or causes you are passionate about. What excites and energizes you?

Identify Your Values

- Consider your core values and beliefs. What principles guide your decisions and actions?

Examine Your Strengths

- Reflect on your strengths and skills. What are you naturally good at, and what do you enjoy doing?

Consider Your Impact

- Think about the impact you want to have on others and the world. How do you want to contribute and make a difference?

Connect with Your Experiences

- Look at your past experiences and achievements. What patterns or themes emerge? What has been most fulfilling for you?

Sarah, a teacher, found her why by reflecting on her passion for education and her desire to make a positive impact on students' lives. Her why became the foundation for her commitment to teaching and helped her stay motivated through the challenges of her profession.

Strategies for Staying Motivated

Once you've identified your why, it's essential to develop strategies to maintain and boost your motivation. Here are some effective strategies:

Set Clear Goals

- Define specific, measurable, achievable, relevant, and time-bound (SMART) goals. Clear goals provide direction and a sense of accomplishment as you achieve them.

Visualize Success

- Regularly visualize yourself achieving your goals. This mental practice reinforces your commitment and boosts motivation.

Break Down Tasks

- Divide large tasks into smaller, manageable chunks. This makes the tasks less overwhelming and allows for steady progress.

Track Your Progress

- Keep a record of your progress toward your goals. Tracking progress provides a sense of accomplishment and highlights how far you've come.

Reward Yourself

- Celebrate small wins and reward yourself for reaching milestones. Rewards provide positive reinforcement and motivation to continue.

Stay Positive

- Maintain a positive mindset and focus on your achievements rather than setbacks. Positive thinking enhances motivation and resilience.

Seek Support

- Surround yourself with supportive people who encourage and motivate you. Share your goals with them and seek their guidance and encouragement.

John, a writer, struggled to stay motivated while working on his novel. By setting clear writing goals, visualizing his book being published, and tracking his daily word count, he was able to stay motivated and complete his manuscript.

Overcoming Motivation Slumps

Even with a clear why and effective strategies, you might still experience periods of low motivation. Here are some tips for overcoming motivation slumps:

Revisit Your Why

- Remind yourself of your deeper purpose and the reasons behind your goals. Reconnecting with your why can reignite your motivation.

Change Your Routine

- Sometimes, a change in routine can help refresh your motivation. Try working in a new environment, adjusting your schedule, or incorporating new activities.

Set Short-Term Goals

- Focus on short-term goals to regain momentum. Achieving small, immediate goals can boost your motivation and confidence.

Practice Self-Care

- Ensure you are taking care of your physical and mental well-being. Rest, exercise, and relaxation are essential for maintaining motivation.

Seek Inspiration

- Find inspiration from books, podcasts, or talks related to your goals. Learning from others' experiences can provide a motivational boost.

Break Tasks into Micro-Tasks

- If a task feels overwhelming, break it down into the smallest possible steps. Completing these micro-tasks can help you gain a sense of progress and motivation.

> *"Success is not the key to happiness. Happiness is the key to success. If you love what you are doing, you will be successful."*
> *– Albert Schweitzer*

J.K. Rowling faced numerous rejections before finding success with the Harry Potter series. Her why—bringing the magical world of Harry Potter to life for readers—kept her motivated through challenges and setbacks.

Elon Musk's motivation to advance technology and make a significant impact on the future drives his ambitious projects, from SpaceX to Tesla. His clear why fuels his perseverance and innovation.

Oprah Winfrey's why centers around empowering others and making a positive impact through storytelling. Her motivation has driven her to build a media empire and become a global icon.

Practical Exercises for Finding and Staying Connected to Your Why

Why Discovery Exercise

- Set aside time for self-reflection. Write down your passions, values, strengths, and desired impact. Identify common themes to discover your why.

Daily Visualization

- Spend a few minutes each day visualizing yourself achieving your goals. Picture the steps you'll take and the satisfaction of reaching your desired outcome.

Goal Setting and Tracking

- Set SMART goals and create a plan to achieve them. Use a journal or app to track your progress and celebrate milestones.

Motivation Journal

- Keep a journal to document your motivations, achievements, and any challenges you encounter. Reflecting on your journey can help you stay connected to your why.

Accountability Partner

- Find an accountability partner who shares similar goals. Regularly check in with each other to share progress, challenges, and motivation.

"The two most important days in your life are the day you are born and the day you find out why."
– Mark Twain

Finding and connecting with your "why" is a powerful tool in overcoming procrastination and achieving your goals. It provides the deep-rooted motivation that can sustain you through challenges and reignite your passion when it wanes.

As Simon Sinek, author of "Start With Why," states, "Working hard for something we don't care about is called stress; working hard for something we love is called passion."

By discovering your purpose, connecting it to your daily tasks, and using it to combat procrastination, you're not just working towards your goals - you're living them. Your "why" transforms the journey from a series of to-do lists into a meaningful pursuit of your deepest aspirations.

Are you ready to find your why and stay motivated to achieve your goals?

19

Overcoming Perfectionism: Embrace Imperfection

"Perfect is overrated. Perfect is boring."
- Tina Fey

Perfectionism, often seen as a desire to achieve excellence, can become a significant barrier to productivity and personal growth. When the pursuit of perfection leads to procrastination, stress, and dissatisfaction, it becomes a hindrance rather than a help. This chapter will explore the nature of perfectionism, its impact on our lives, and strategies for overcoming it. By embracing imperfection and focusing on progress rather than perfection, you can enhance your productivity and well-being.

Understanding Perfectionism

Perfectionism is characterized by setting excessively high standards for oneself and striving for flawlessness. While aiming for high standards can be motivating, perfectionism often leads to negative outcomes:

1. Procrastination: Fear of not meeting high standards can cause delays in starting or completing tasks.
2. Stress and Anxiety: Constant pressure to be perfect can lead to chronic stress and anxiety.
3. Reduced Productivity: Excessive attention to detail can slow down progress and reduce overall productivity.
4. Low Self-Esteem: Perfectionists often tie their self-worth to their achievements, leading to self-criticism and low self-esteem.
5. Fear of Failure: The fear of making mistakes or failing can prevent taking risks and trying new things.

The Costs of Perfectionism

While perfectionism may seem admirable, its consequences can be severe:

1. Reduced productivity: Perfectionists often spend excessive time on minor details, hindering overall progress.
2. Increased stress and anxiety: The constant pressure to be perfect can lead to burnout and mental health issues.
3. Impaired creativity: Fear of making mistakes stifles innovation and risk-taking.
4. Strained relationships: Unrealistic expectations can

create tension with colleagues, friends, and family.
5. Missed opportunities: Perfectionism can prevent people from taking on new challenges or pursuing goals.

Strategies for Overcoming Perfectionism

Recognize and challenge perfectionistic thoughts
Start by identifying perfectionistic thoughts and beliefs. When you notice them, challenge these ideas with more realistic and compassionate alternatives.
Example:
Perfectionistic thought: "If this presentation isn't flawless, I'm a complete failure."
Challenge: "Even if the presentation isn't perfect, it can still be valuable and well-received. My worth isn't determined by a single performance."

Set realistic and flexible goals
Instead of aiming for perfection, set achievable goals that allow for growth and learning. Embrace the concept of "good enough" and focus on progress rather than perfection.
Example: Rather than expecting to master a new skill immediately, set a goal to practice consistently and improve over time.

Practice self-compassion
Treat yourself with the same kindness and understanding you would offer a friend. Acknowledge that mistakes and setbacks are part of the human experience and opportunities for growth.

As researcher Dr. Kristin Neff explains, "Self-compassion involves treating yourself with the same kindness, concern, and support you'd show to a good friend."

Embrace the growth mindset

Adopt a growth mindset, which views challenges and failures as opportunities to learn and improve, rather than as reflections of fixed abilities.

Example: Instead of thinking, "I'm not good at public speaking," reframe it as "I'm still learning and improving my public speaking skills."

Focus on the process, not just the outcome

Shift your attention from the end result to the journey of learning and growth. Celebrate small victories and progress along the way.

Example: When working on a project, acknowledge and appreciate the skills you're developing and the insights you're gaining, regardless of the final outcome.

Practice mindfulness

Mindfulness can help you stay present and reduce anxiety about future outcomes. It allows you to observe perfectionistic thoughts without getting caught up in them.

Try this simple mindfulness exercise:
- Take a few deep breaths
- Notice any perfectionistic thoughts or feelings
- Acknowledge them without judgment
- Gently redirect your focus to the present moment

Embrace imperfection in daily life

Intentionally allow for small imperfections in your daily routine to build tolerance for imperfection.

Examples:
- Leave a small area of your desk unorganized
- Send an email without proofreading it multiple times
- Wear mismatched socks

Reframe mistakes as learning opportunities

Instead of viewing mistakes as failures, see them as valuable lessons that contribute to your growth and development.
As author Neil Gaiman advises, "Make glorious, amazing mistakes. Make mistakes nobody's ever made before. Don't freeze, don't stop, don't worry that it isn't good enough, or it isn't perfect, whatever it is: art, or love, or work or family or life."

Set time limits and deadlines

Establish reasonable time constraints for tasks to prevent excessive perfectionism from slowing you down.

Example: When writing a report, set a specific deadline and stick to it, even if you feel it's not perfect.

Seek feedback and alternative perspectives

Ask trusted friends, colleagues, or mentors for honest feedback. Their perspectives can help you gain a more balanced view of your work and abilities.

Example: Share a draft of your work with a colleague and ask for constructive criticism, focusing on areas for improvement rather than perfection.

Challenge the all-or-nothing thinking

Perfectionism often involves black-and-white thinking. Practice recognizing shades of gray and partial successes.
Example: Instead of seeing a project as either a complete success or total failure, acknowledge the aspects that went well while identifying areas for future improvement.

Celebrate effort and progress
Shift your focus from outcomes to the effort and progress you've made. Recognize that consistent effort leads to improvement over time.

As author Zig Ziglar said, "You don't have to be great to start, but you have to start to be great."

Practice selective perfectionism
Identify areas where high standards are truly necessary and areas where "good enough" is sufficient. This allows you to allocate your energy more effectively.
Example: You might maintain very high standards for critical work presentations but allow for more flexibility in daily email communications.

Develop a growth narrative
Create a personal story that emphasizes growth, learning, and resilience rather than perfect performance.
Example: "My journey is about continuous improvement and embracing challenges, not about being flawless."

Expose yourself to imperfection
Intentionally engage in activities where perfectionism is impossible or counterproductive.
Examples:

- Try a new hobby where you're a complete beginner
- Participate in improvisational activities
- Engage in collaborative projects where you can't control every aspect

> *"Perfection is not attainable, but if we chase perfection, we can catch excellence."*
> *– Vince Lombardi*

Jane found herself constantly revising her work to meet her impossibly high standards. This led to missed deadlines, increased stress, and a decline in her overall job satisfaction. By learning to embrace imperfection, she was able to complete projects more efficiently and reduce her stress levels.

Strategies for Overcoming Perfectionism

Overcoming perfectionism involves changing your mindset and adopting healthier habits. Here are some strategies to help you embrace imperfection:

Set Realistic Goals

- Set achievable and realistic goals. Break tasks into smaller, manageable steps and focus on progress rather than perfection.

Challenge Perfectionistic Thoughts

- Recognize and challenge perfectionistic thoughts. Replace them with more realistic and compassionate self-talk.

Practice Self-Compassion

- Treat yourself with the same kindness and understanding you would offer a friend. Acknowledge that everyone makes mistakes and that imperfection is part of being human.

Focus on Effort, Not Outcomes

- Shift your focus from the end result to the effort and process. Celebrate your efforts and progress, regardless of the outcome.

Set Time Limits

- Allocate a specific amount of time to complete tasks. Avoid spending excessive time on minor details by setting deadlines for yourself.

Embrace Mistakes as Learning Opportunities

- View mistakes as opportunities for learning and growth. Understand that mistakes are a natural part of the learning process.

Seek Feedback

- Seek constructive feedback from others. Use it to improve rather than as a measure of your worth.

Limit Comparisons

- Avoid comparing yourself to others. Focus on your own progress and achievements.

Tom, an entrepreneur, struggled with perfectionism in his business ventures. By setting realistic goals, practicing self-compassion, and viewing mistakes as learning opportunities, he was able to overcome his perfectionistic tendencies and achieve greater success.

Practical Exercises to Embrace Imperfection

Daily Gratitude Journal

- Keep a journal to write down three things you're grateful for each day. This practice helps shift your focus from perfection to appreciation of what you have achieved.

Progress Over Perfection

- At the end of each day, write down what you accomplished, focusing on progress rather than perfection. Reflect on how small steps contribute to your larger goals.

Self-Compassion Meditation

- Practice self-compassion meditation to cultivate kindness and understanding towards yourself. Guided meditations can help you develop a more compassionate mindset.

Mistake Log

- Keep a log of mistakes you make and write down what you learned from each one. This helps you view mistakes as valuable learning experiences.

Feedback Loop

- Regularly seek feedback on your work and use it to make improvements. Focus on constructive feedback rather than seeking validation.

> *"Have no fear of perfection – you'll never reach it."*
> *– Salvador Dalí*

Laura, a perfectionist student, feared submitting imperfect assignments. By gradually allowing herself to submit work that wasn't perfect and seeking support from her professors, she overcame her fear and improved her academic performance.

Overcoming perfectionism is a journey that requires patience, self-compassion, and consistent effort. By embracing imperfection, you open yourself to greater creativity, resilience, and fulfillment. Remember that perfection is an illusion, and true growth comes from embracing the messy, imperfect process of learning and development.

By letting go of the need for perfection, you create space for authenticity, innovation, and meaningful connections. Embrace your imperfections as unique aspects of your journey, and allow yourself the freedom to grow, learn, and thrive in a world that is beautifully imperfect.

Are you ready to let go of perfectionism and embrace the power of imperfection?

20

Using Mindfulness: Stay Present and Focused

"Mindfulness is a way of befriending ourselves and our experience."
– Jon Kabat-Zinn

In today's fast-paced world, distractions are everywhere, and staying present and focused can be a challenge. Mindfulness, the practice of being fully aware and engaged in the present moment, offers a powerful solution. This chapter explores how mindfulness can enhance focus, reduce stress, and improve overall well-being. By incorporating mindfulness into your daily routine, you can stay present, boost your productivity, and lead a more fulfilling life.

What is Mindfulness?

Mindfulness is rooted in ancient Buddhist meditation practices but has gained widespread popularity in recent years due to its scientifically proven benefits. Mindfulness is the practice of paying attention to the present moment with an open and non-judgmental attitude. It involves being aware of your thoughts, feelings, and sensations as they arise, without getting caught up in them. Mindfulness can be cultivated through various techniques, including meditation, breathing exercises, and mindful awareness in daily activities.

> *"Mindfulness is the aware, balanced acceptance of the present experience. It isn't more complicated than that."*
> *– Sylvia Boorstein*

The Benefits of Mindfulness

Mindfulness offers numerous benefits for both mental and physical health:

Improved Focus and Concentration

- Regular mindfulness practice enhances your ability to focus and concentrate on tasks by training your mind to stay in the present moment.

Reduced Stress and Anxiety

- Mindfulness reduces stress and anxiety by helping you become more aware of your thoughts and emotions, allowing you to respond to them more effectively.

Enhanced Emotional Regulation

- Mindfulness improves emotional regulation by increasing awareness of your emotional responses and promoting a more balanced reaction.

Better Decision Making

- Being present and aware helps you make more thoughtful and informed decisions, free from the influence of automatic reactions and biases.

Increased Resilience

- Mindfulness builds resilience by promoting a sense of calm and stability, even in the face of challenges and adversity.

Techniques for Cultivating Mindfulness

Mindful Breathing
One of the simplest and most effective mindfulness techniques is focused breathing:
   - Find a comfortable position and close your eyes
   - Focus your attention on your breath
   - Notice the sensation of air moving in and out of your nostrils or the rise and fall of your chest
   - When your mind wanders (which it will), gently bring your attention back to your breath

- Start with 5 minutes and gradually increase the duration

Body Scan Meditation
This practice involves systematically focusing your attention on different parts of your body: - Lie down or sit comfortably - Starting from your toes, focus your attention on each part

of your body, moving upward
- Notice any sensations, tension, or discomfort without trying to change anything
- If your mind wanders, gently bring it back to the body part you're focusing on

Mindful Walking
This technique involves bringing awareness to the act of walking:
- Walk at a natural pace
- Pay attention to the sensation of your feet touching the ground
- Notice the movement of your legs, arms, and body
- Observe your surroundings without getting caught up in thoughts about them

Mindful Eating
Bring mindfulness to your meals by:
- Eating slowly and without distractions
- Noticing the colors, smells, textures, and tastes of your food
- Paying attention to your body's hunger and fullness cues

The STOP Technique

Use this quick mindfulness practice throughout your day:
- Stop what you're doing
- Take a few deep breaths
- Observe your thoughts, feelings, and bodily sensations
- Proceed with awareness

Incorporating Mindfulness into Daily Life

Start Your Day Mindfully
Begin each morning with a short mindfulness practice. This could be a few minutes of mindful breathing or a body scan meditation.

Use Transition Times
Use the time between activities (e.g., before starting work, during your commute) to practice mindfulness.

Create Mindful Reminders
Set alarms on your phone or place sticky notes in visible locations to remind yourself to take mindful moments throughout the day.

Practice Mindful Listening
When in conversation, give your full attention to the speaker. Notice when your mind wanders and gently bring it back to the conversation.

Engage in Mindful Work
Bring full attention to your tasks, focusing on one thing at a time rather than multitasking.

End Your Day Mindfully
Take a few minutes before bed to reflect on your day without judgment, acknowledging both challenges and positive moments.

Overcoming Common Challenges in Mindfulness Practice

"I Don't Have Time"
Remember that even a few minutes of mindfulness can be beneficial. Start small and gradually increase your practice time.

"My Mind Won't Stop Wandering"
Mind-wandering is normal and part of the process. The practice is in noticing when your mind has wandered and gently bringing it back to the present.

"I'm Not Doing It Right"
There's no "right" way to practice mindfulness. The key is consistency and a non-judgmental attitude towards your practice.

"I Feel Restless or Uncomfortable"
Physical discomfort or restlessness is common, especially for beginners. Notice these sensations without judgment and return to your point of focus.

"I'm Not Seeing Results"
Mindfulness benefits often accumulate subtly over time.

Trust in the process and be patient with yourself.

Emma found herself constantly distracted by emails and social media notifications. By practicing mindfulness meditation for just 10 minutes each morning, she was able to improve her focus, reduce stress, and enhance her productivity at work.

John started incorporating mindful walking into his daily routine. By taking a 10-minute walk during his lunch break and focusing on his surroundings, he felt more refreshed and focused when he returned to work.

Lisa, a busy mother and teacher, found it challenging to balance her responsibilities. By integrating mindfulness into her daily routine, she was able to manage stress better, stay focused on her tasks, and enjoy more meaningful interactions with her family.

Mark, a high school student, struggled with staying focused during mindfulness meditation. By starting with just three minutes of mindful breathing each day and gradually increasing the time, he developed a more consistent practice and improved his concentration.

Mindfulness is a powerful practice that can help you stay present, focused, and improve your overall well-being. By incorporating mindfulness into your daily routine, you can enhance your productivity, reduce stress, and lead a more fulfilling life. Start with small steps, be patient with yourself, and embrace the journey of becoming more mindful. Remember, the present moment is the only moment you have, so make the most of it.

In the words of Thich Nhat Hanh, "The present moment is filled with joy and happiness. If you are attentive, you will see it." Through mindfulness, we can tap into this joy and happiness, transforming our experience of life one moment at a time.

Are you ready to embrace mindfulness and stay present and focused in your daily life?

21

Building a Support Network: Surround Yourself with Positive People

"Surround yourself with only people who are going to lift you higher."
– Oprah Winfrey

A strong support network is crucial for personal and professional growth. Positive relationships provide encouragement, motivation, and constructive feedback, helping you stay focused and resilient. This chapter explores the importance of building a support network and offers practical strategies for surrounding yourself with positive, supportive individuals.

The Importance of a Support Network

Having a support network offers numerous benefits:

Emotional Support

- Friends and family provide a listening ear and emotional comfort during challenging times.

Motivation and Encouragement

- Supportive individuals encourage you to pursue your goals and overcome obstacles.

Accountability

- A support network holds you accountable for your actions and helps you stay on track.

Diverse Perspectives

- Different viewpoints and experiences can provide valuable insights and solutions to problems.

Improved Well-Being

- Positive social connections enhance mental and physical health, reducing stress and promoting happiness.

As motivational speaker Jim Rohn famously said, "You are the average of the five people you spend the most time with." This underscores the significant impact that our social circle can have on our mindset, behavior, and overall quality of life.

Strategies for Building a Positive Support Network

Identify your current network
   Start by assessing your existing relationships. Consider:
      - Who do you spend most of your time with?
      - Who do you turn to when you need support?
      - Who leaves you feeling energized and positive after interactions?
      - Who tends to drain your energy or bring negativity into your life?
   This evaluation will help you recognize the positive influences in your life and areas where you might need to make changes.

Define your values and goals
   Clarity about your own values and goals will help you connect with like-minded individuals. Ask yourself:
      - What are my core values?
      - What are my short-term and long-term goals?
      - What kind of support do I need to achieve these goals?

Cultivate existing positive relationships
   Strengthen bonds with those who already bring positivity to your life. This might involve:
      - Scheduling regular catch-ups
      - Showing appreciation for their support
      - Being there for them when they need support
      - Engaging in shared interests or activities

Seek out new connections

Expand your network by actively seeking new positive relationships. Some ways to do this include:
- Joining clubs or groups aligned with your interests
- Attending networking events in your field
- Volunteering for causes you care about
- Taking classes or workshops to learn new skills
- Using social media and professional networking platforms

Remember, quality is more important than quantity. As author Marian Wright Edelman notes, "It's time for greatness — not for greed. It's a time for idealism — not ideology. It's a time not just for compassionate words, but compassionate action."

Be open and approachable

Cultivate an open and friendly demeanor to attract positive people. This includes:
  - Practicing active listening
  - Showing genuine interest in others
  - Being willing to share about yourself
  - Maintaining a positive attitude

Set boundaries with negative influences

While it's important to be compassionate, it's equally crucial to protect your energy from consistently negative or toxic individuals. This might involve:
  - Limiting time spent with negative people
  - Setting clear boundaries about acceptable behavior
  - Redirecting conversations to more positive topics
  - In some cases, distancing yourself from highly toxic relationships

Nurture reciprocal relationships

Build relationships based on mutual support and respect. This involves:
- Being there for others when they need support
- Celebrating others' successes
- Offering help and resources when you can
- Being willing to both give and receive support

Diversify your network

A diverse network can provide a range of perspectives and types of support. Consider connecting with people who:
- Are from different cultural backgrounds
- Have varied professional experiences
- Are at different life stages
- Have diverse skill sets and areas of expertise

Leverage technology

Use technology to maintain and expand your support network:
- Stay in touch with distant friends and family through video calls
- Join online communities related to your interests or profession
- Use apps designed for meeting new friends or networking

Invest time in your relationships

Building a strong support network requires consistent effort. Make time for your relationships, even when life gets busy. As leadership expert John C. Maxwell says, "The greatest good you can do for another is not just to share your riches but to reveal to him his own."

Practice gratitude

Regularly express appreciation for the positive people in your life. This can strengthen your relationships and attract more positivity. Consider:
- Sending thank-you notes
- Verbalizing your appreciation
- Performing acts of kindness for those who support you

Be the positive influence you seek

Embody the qualities you want to attract in others. This includes:
- Maintaining a positive outlook
- Offering support and encouragement to others
- Avoiding gossip and negative talk
- Demonstrating integrity and reliability

Examples of Positive Support Networks

Professional Mentorship Programs

Many companies and professional organizations offer mentorship programs that pair experienced professionals with those seeking guidance. These relationships can provide valuable support, advice, and networking opportunities within a specific field.

Support Groups

Support groups bring together individuals facing similar challenges, whether it's a health issue, life transition, or shared goal. These groups provide a safe space for sharing experiences, offering mutual support, and gaining different perspectives.

Mastermind Groups
Popularized by Napoleon Hill in his book "Think and Grow Rich," mastermind groups consist of peers who meet regularly to share goals, challenges, and support each other's growth. These groups can be particularly effective for entrepreneurs and professionals seeking to accelerate their personal and professional development.

Online Communities
   Platforms like Reddit, Facebook Groups, and industry-specific forums allow people to connect with others who share similar interests or experiences. These communities can provide a sense of belonging and support, especially for those who might feel isolated in their immediate environment.

Accountability Partnerships
   Pairing up with an accountability partner can provide mutual support in achieving goals. This could be a workout buddy, a fellow entrepreneur, or someone working towards similar personal development objectives.

Overcoming Challenges in Building a Support Network

Social Anxiety
   For those who struggle with social anxiety, building a support network can feel daunting. Start small:
   - Begin with one-on-one interactions
   - Practice self-compassion
   - Consider seeking professional help to develop coping

strategies

Limited Time

In our busy lives, it can be challenging to find time for relationship-building. Prioritize by:
 - Scheduling regular check-ins with important contacts
 - Combining socializing with other activities (e.g., exercising with a friend)
 - Using commute time for phone catch-ups

Geographic Isolation

For those living in remote areas or frequently relocating, maintaining a support network can be challenging. Strategies include:
 - Leveraging online communities and video calls
 - Joining local groups or classes to meet people in new locations
 - Maintaining long-distance friendships through regular communication

Difficulty Opening Up

Building deep connections requires vulnerability. If you struggle with this:
 - Start by sharing small things and gradually build trust
 - Practice active listening to encourage others to open up
 - Remember that vulnerability often strengthens relationships

Sarah, a college student, realized that her friends were often negative and unsupportive of her academic goals. By seeking out classmates who shared her dedication to studying and personal growth, she built a new support network that motivated her to excel.

David, an aspiring entrepreneur, joined a local startup commu- nity and attended networking events. By actively participating and engaging with others, he built a network of supportive fellow entrepreneurs who offered advice and encouragement.

Nurturing Positive Relationships

Building a support network is just the beginning; nurturing these relationships is equally important. Here are some tips for maintaining and strengthening your connections:

Communicate Regularly

- Stay in touch with your support network through regular communication. Use phone calls, texts, emails, or social media to keep connected.

Offer Support in Return

- Support is a two-way street. Offer your help and encouragement to others in your network.

Express Gratitude

- Show appreciation for the support you receive. A simple thank you or a thoughtful gesture can strengthen your relationships.

Be Present and Attentive

- Whenspendingtimewithyoursupportnetwork,befully present and attentive. Listen actively and engage in meaningful conversations.

Celebrate Achievements

- Celebrate the successes and milestones of those in your network. Recognize their achievements and share in their joy.

Emily, a writer, made it a point to regularly check in with her writing group. By offering feedback on their work and celebrating their successes, she fostered a supportive and collaborative environment.

James, an introverted graphic designer, found it difficult to network at large events. By joining a small local art group, he was able to build meaningful connections in a more comfortable setting.

> *"The people we surround ourselves with either raise or lower our standards. They either help us become the best version of ourselves or encourage us to become lesser versions of ourselves."*
> *– Anonymous*

Building a support network and surrounding yourself with positive people is essential for personal and professional growth. By identifying the right individuals, actively building connections, and nurturing relationships, you can create a strong and supportive network. Embrace the power of positive relationships and let them lift you to new heights.

As motivational speaker Zig Ziglar wisely said, "You don't have to be great to start, but you have to start to be great." Begin today by taking small steps to nurture existing positive relationships and open yourself to new connections. Remember, the quality of your relationships significantly influences the quality of your life. Invest in building a positive support network, and you'll find yourself better equipped to face life's challenges and celebrate its joys.

Are you ready to build your support network and surround yourself with positive people?

22

Creating a Vision Board: Visualize Success

"Visualization is daydreaming with a purpose."
– Bo Bennett

Visualization is a powerful tool that can help you achieve your goals by creating a clear and compelling image of your desired future. A vision board is a visual representation of your goals and aspirations, serving as a constant reminder of what you're working towards. This chapter explores how to create a vision board and use it to visualize success, helping you stay focused and motivated.

The Power of Visualization

Visualization involves creating a mental image of a desired outcome. When you visualize your goals, you engage your brain in a way that makes your aspirations feel more attainable. This practice can enhance motivation, increase focus, and improve performance.

Understanding Vision Boards

A vision board, also known as a dream board or goal board, is a collage of images, quotes, and affirmations that represent your goals and dreams. It's a visual tool that helps clarify, concentrate, and maintain focus on specific life goals. The idea behind a vision board is based on the Law of Attraction - the belief that by focusing on positive or negative thoughts, people can bring positive or negative experiences into their lives.

Benefits of Creating a Vision Board

1. Clarity of goals: The process of creating a vision board helps you clarify what you truly want in life.
2. Increasedfocus: Avisionboardservesasadailyreminder of your goals, helping you stay focused on what's important.
3. Motivation: Visualizing your goals can boost motivation and inspire action towards achieving them.
4. Positivemindset: Focusingonyouraspirationspromotes a positive outlook on life.
5. Subconscious programming: Regular visualization can influence your subconscious mind to work towards your goals.
6. Creativity boost: The process of creating a vision board can stimulate creativity and new ideas.

As Oprah Winfrey, a known advocate of vision boards, says, "Create the highest, grandest vision possible for your life, because you become what you believe."

Steps to Create an Effective Vision Board

Reflect on Your Goals
Before you start creating your vision board, take time to reflect on your goals and aspirations. Consider various areas of your life:
- Career and finances
- Relationships and family
- Personal growth and education
- Health and fitness
- Spirituality and mindfulness
- Travel and adventures
- Hobbies and interests

Gather Materials
  Collect the following materials:
- A large poster board or corkboard
- Magazines, newspapers, printed images
- Scissors
- Glue or tape
- Markers or pens
- Optional: decorative elements like stickers, ribbons, etc.

Find Inspiring Images and Words
  Browse through magazines and online resources to find images and words that resonate with your goals. Look for:
- Pictures that represent your goals
- Inspiring quotes or affirmations

- Words that encapsulate your aspirations

Remember, there's no right or wrong - choose what speaks to you personally.

Arrange and Attach

Once you have your materials, start arranging them on your board. Consider the following:
- Group related items together
- Place your most important goals in the center or prominent positions
- Create a pleasing visual layout

When you're satisfied with the arrangement, glue or tape everything in place.

Add Personal Touches

Personalize your vision board with:
- Your own photos
- Hand-written goals or affirmations
- Small objects or trinkets that represent your dreams

Display Your Vision Board

Place your completed vision board where you'll see it daily, such as:
- Your bedroom wall
- Your office desk
- As a screensaver on your computer or phone

Engage with Your Vision Board Regularly

Make it a habit to look at and engage with your vision board:
- Spend a few minutes each morning visualizing your goals
- Reflect on your progress regularly

- Update your board as you achieve goals or your aspirations evolve

Examples of Effective Vision Boards

Career Success Vision Board
A vision board focused on career success might include:
- Images of your dream job or office
- Logos of companies you'd like to work for
- Income goals represented by images of wealth
- Quotes about success and hard work
- Skills you want to develop

Health and Wellness Vision Board
A health-focused vision board could feature:
- Images of healthy foods
- Pictures of people engaged in exercises you enjoy
- Quotes about health and vitality
- Images representing your ideal body or fitness level
- Words like "strength," "energy," and "balance"

Personal Growth Vision Board
A personal development vision board might include:
- Books you want to read - Skills you want to learn - Places you want to travel for personal enrichment - Quotes about wisdom and growth - Images representing peace and mindfulness

Tips for Maximizing the Impact of Your Vision Board

Be Specific
The more specific your images and goals, the more powerful your vision board will be. Instead of a generic image of a house, find a picture that closely resembles your dream home.

Include a Mix of Short-term and Long-term Goals
Balance your vision board with both immediate and future aspirations to maintain motivation over time.

Use "I Am" Statements
Frame your goals as if you've already achieved them. For example, "I am confident" or "I am financially free."

Engage Multiple Senses
While vision boards are primarily visual, consider how you can engage other senses. For example, you might add a fabric swatch to represent the texture of your dream car's seats.

Make it a Ritual
Create a ritual around your vision board. This could involve spending a few minutes each morning visualizing your goals or meditating in front of your board.

Be Open to Possibilities
While it's good to be specific, also leave room for unexpected opportunities. As author Martha Beck advises, "The way to create a vision for your life that actually comes true is to create a vision that's so vague you couldn't possibly miss it."

Believe in Your Vision

Cultivate genuine belief in the possibilities represented on your board. As Henry Ford famously said, "Whether you think you can, or you think you can't – you're right."

Overcoming Common Challenges

1. LackofClarity: Ifyou'reunsureaboutyourgoals,start with broad themes and refine as you gain clarity.
2. Overwhelm: If you have too many goals, prioritize and focus on the most important ones for now.
3. Skepticism: If you're skeptical about vision boards, approach it as an experiment. Give it a genuine try and observe the results.
4. Impatience: Remember that change takes time. Trust the process and stay consistent in your efforts.

Samantha, a freelance graphic designer, created a vision board filled with images of successful projects, happy clients, and her dream workspace. This daily reminder kept her motivated and focused on growing her business.

Mark, an aspiring author, created a vision board with images of best-selling books, writing retreats, and inspiring quotes from his favorite authors. Displaying it in his writing nook kept him motivated to write every day.

Emily, a fitness enthusiast, used her vision board to visualize her fitness goals. She set weekly workout intentions and read affirmations about her strength and resilience. Her vision board kept her motivated to stay on track with her fitness routine.

John, a business owner, initially struggled with negative self-talk about his ability to expand his company. By incorporating daily affirmations and visualizing his success, he gradually built confidence and saw significant business growth.

Practical Exercises for Creating and Using a Vision Board

Goal Setting Exercise

- Write down your short-term and long-term goals. Be specific and think about different areas of your life.

Visualization Meditation

- Spend five minutes each day visualizing yourself achieving your goals. Focus on the details and the emotions associated with your success.

Affirmation Writing

- Write positive affirmations related to your goals. Read them aloud while looking at your vision board.

Creative Collage Making

- Set aside time to gather images and create your vision board. Enjoy the creative process and let your intuition guide you.

Vision Board Journal

- Keep a journal where you document your progress, reflect on your visualization practice, and note any updates to your vision board.

> *"The more you see it, the more you believe it. The more you believe it, the more you achieve it."*
> *– Unknown*

Creating a vision board is a powerful step towards manifesting your dreams and goals. It serves as a daily reminder of what you're working towards and can help align your actions with your aspirations. Remember, a vision board is not magic – it's a tool to inspire action and maintain focus.

By regularly engaging with your vision board, you're programming your mind to recognize opportunities and take actions that align with your goals. Whether you're aiming for career success, personal growth, or a balanced life, a well-crafted vision board can be your compass, guiding you towards your ideal future.

Start creating your vision board today, and take the first step towards turning your dreams into reality. Remember, the future belongs to those who believe in the beauty of their dreams and take consistent action to achieve them.

Are you ready to create your vision board and visualize your success?

23

Using Positive Self-Talk: Encourage Yourself

"Whether you think you can, or you think you can't – you're right."
– Henry Ford

Positive self-talk is a powerful tool that can transform your mindset and influence your actions. By speaking to yourself in a kind, encouraging way, you can boost your confidence, improve your mood, and enhance your overall performance. This chapter explores the concept of positive self-talk, its benefits, and practical strategies to incorporate it into your daily life.

UnderstandingSelf-Talk

Self-talk refers to the internal narrative we maintain about ourselves, our abilities, and the world around us. It can be positive, negative, or neutral, and it significantly influences our self-esteem, confidence, and performance.

The Science Behind Positive Self-Talk

Positive self-talk involves making affirming, constructive comments to yourself. This practice can counteract negative thoughts and build a healthier, more resilient mindset. Research has shown that positive self-talk can improve mental health, enhance performance, and reduce stress.

Benefits of Positive Self-Talk

Improved Self-Esteem

- Positive self-talk enhances your self-image and self-worth, helping you feel more confident in your abilities.

Increased Motivation

- Encouraging words can boost your motivation and drive, making it easier to pursue your goals.

Reduced Stress

- By focusing on positive thoughts, you can reduce anxiety and stress, promoting a calmer and more balanced mindset.

Enhanced Performance

- Positive self-talk can improve your performance in various areas, from academics to sports to work.

Better Resilience

- Encouraging yourself helps you bounce back from setbacks and challenges more effectively.

The Impact of Negative Self-Talk

Negative self-talk can:

1. Increase stress and anxiety
2. Lower self-esteem and confidence
3. Limit potential and hinder goal achievement
4. Contribute to depression and other mental health issues
5. Negatively affect relationships and social interactions

Recognizing Negative Self-Talk Patterns

Common forms of negative self-talk include:

All-or-Nothing Thinking: Seeing things in black and white categories.
Example: "If I'm not perfect, I'm a total failure."

Overgeneralization: Drawing broad conclusions from a single event.
Example: "I failed one test, so I'll never succeed in this subject."

Mental Filtering: Focusing solely on negative aspects while

ignoring positives.
   Example: Dwelling on one criticism amidst numerous compliments.

Jumping to Conclusions: Making negative interpretations without supporting facts.
   Example: "He didn't smile at me. He must not like me."

Catastrophizing: Anticipating the worst possible outcome.
   Example: "If I make a mistake in my presentation, my career will be over."

Personalization: Blaming yourself for events beyond your control.
   Example: "The project failed because I'm not good enough."

Should Statements: Using rigid, unrealistic expectations.
   Example: "I should always be happy and never make mistakes."

Transforming Negative Self-Talk into Positive Self-Encouragement

Awareness: The First Step
   Start by becoming aware of your self-talk. Pay attention to your internal dialogue throughout the day. Consider keeping a journal to track recurring thoughts and patterns.

Challenge Negative Thoughts
   When you notice negative self-talk, pause and challenge it:

- Is this thought based on facts or assumptions?
- What evidence contradicts this negative thought?
- How would I advise a friend in this situation?

Reframe Negative Statements

Practice turning negative statements into positive or neutral ones:

Negative: "I'm terrible at public speaking."

Reframed: "Public speaking is a skill I'm working on improving."

Use Affirmations

Develop positive affirmations to counter negative self-talk:
- "I am capable of handling challenges."
- "I learn and grow from my experiences."
- "I am worthy of success and happiness."

Repeat these affirmations regularly, especially when facing self-doubt.

Practice Self-Compassion

Treat yourself with the same kindness you'd offer a good friend. When you make a mistake or face a setback, respond with understanding and encouragement rather than harsh criticism.

Focus on Growth and Learning

Adopt a growth mindset by viewing challenges as opportunities for learning and improvement. Replace "I can't" with "I can't yet, but I'm learning."

Use "You" Instead of "I"

Research suggests that using second-person pronouns in self-talk can be more effective. For example, instead of "I can do this," try "You can do this."

Visualize Success
Use your inner voice to vividly imagine successful outcomes. Describe to yourself in detail how you'll overcome challenges and achieve your goals.

Celebrate Small Wins
Acknowledge and praise yourself for small accomplishments. This builds confidence and motivates further progress.

Practice Gratitude
Regularly express gratitude for positive aspects of your life. This shifts focus from what's lacking to what's abundant.

Techniques for Cultivating Positive Self-Talk

The Mirror Technique
Stand in front of a mirror and speak encouraging words to yourself. This might feel awkward at first but can be a powerful way to internalize positive messages.

Create a Personal Mantra
Develop a short, powerful phrase that resonates with you and repeat it regularly. For example: "I am resilient and capable."

Write Letters to Yourself
Compose encouraging letters to yourself, offering support

and advice as you would to a dear friend.

Use Positive Reminders
Place sticky notes with uplifting messages in visible locations or set encouraging reminders on your phone.

Practice Positive Self-Talk During Exercise
Use encouraging self-talk during physical activities to push through challenges and improve performance.

Develop a Pre-Performance Routine
Before important events or challenging tasks, engage in a brief positive self-talk routine to boost confidence and focus.

Create a Success Journal
Regularly record your achievements, no matter how small, to build a repository of positive experiences to reflect on.

Overcoming Challenges in Developing Positive Self-Talk

Persistence of Negative Patterns
Changing long-standing thought patterns takes time and consistent effort. Be patient with yourself and celebrate small improvements.

Feeling Inauthentic
Initially, positive self-talk might feel forced or insincere. Remember that you're learning a new skill, and it will become more natural with practice.

Setbacks and Disappointments

During challenging times, it's easy to revert to negative self-talk. Use these moments as opportunities to practice resilience and self-compassion.

Perfectionism

Avoid the trap of expecting perfect positive thinking. Allow for a balanced, realistic perspective that acknowledges challenges while maintaining an overall positive outlook.

> *"The way you talk to yourself can either move you forward or hold you back. Choose to speak words that empower and inspire."*
> *– Unknown*

Lisa, a competitive swimmer, used positive self-talk to boost her confidence before races. By repeating affirmations like "I am strong and capable," she improved her performance and achieved personal bests.

Types of Self-Talk

Self-talk can be categorized into several types:

Affirmations

- Positive statements about yourself and your abilities, such as "I am capable of achieving my goals."

Instructional Self-Talk

- Directing yourself with specific instructions to improve

performance, like "Stay focused and keep a steady pace."

Motivational Self-Talk

- Encouraging phrases that boost your motivation, such as "I can do this" or "Keep going, you're almost there."

Reflective Self-Talk

- Reflecting on past experiences and learning from them in a positive way, like "I handled that situation well and can do it again."

John, a public speaker, used instructional self-talk to stay focused during his presentations. By mentally rehearsing phrases like "Speak slowly and clearly," he delivered more effective speeches.

Maria, a college student, struggled with negative self-talk during exams. By identifying her negative thoughts and replacing them with affirmations like "I have prepared well and am capable," she reduced her anxiety and improved her test performance.

David, an aspiring musician, used the mirror exercise to boost his confidence before performances. By looking at himself and saying "I am talented and ready to shine," he felt more assured on stage.

Overcoming Challenges in Positive Self-Talk

While developing positive self-talk can be transformative, it may also come with challenges. Here are some common obstacles and how to overcome them:

Deep-Seated Negative Beliefs

- If you have long-held negative beliefs, it may take time and consistent effort to change them. Be patient with yourself and seek professional help if needed.

External Negative Influences

- Surround yourself with positive influences and minimize exposure to negative people or environments that undermine your efforts.

Inconsistent Practice

- Make positive self-talk a regular part of your routine. Set reminders or incorporate it into daily activities like brushing your teeth or commuting.

Impatience

- Understand that changing your self-talk is a gradual process. Celebrate small victories and progress along the way.

Self-Doubt

- Counteract self-doubt by focusing on your strengths and past successes. Remind yourself of times when you overcame challenges.

Karen, a software developer, struggled with deep-seated negative beliefs about her abilities. By consistently practicing positive self-talk and seeking support from a mentor, she gradually built confidence and advanced in her career.

Your inner voice can be your strongest ally or your worst critic. By cultivating positive self-talk, you create a supportive internal environment that fosters growth, resilience, and success. Remember, the way you talk to yourself matters immensely.

Positive self-talk is a powerful tool that can transform your mindset and influence your actions. By speaking to yourself in an encouraging and constructive way, you can boost your confidence, reduce stress, and improve your overall performance. Embrace the power of positive self-talk and let it guide you towards achieving your goals.

Are you ready to start using positive self-talk to encourage yourself?

24

Embracing Failure: Learn from Your Mistakes

"Failure is simply the opportunity to begin again, this time more intelligently."
– Henry Ford

Failure is an inevitable part of life, yet it is often viewed negatively. Embracing failure means recognizing it as an opportunity for growth and learning rather than a setback. This chapter explores how to reframe your perspective on failure, learn from your mistakes, and use these experiences to propel yourself toward success.

Redefining Failure

Failure is often seen as a dead end, but in reality, it's a stepping stone to success. It's a sign that you are trying, learning, and growing. By redefining failure as a valuable learning experience, you can develop resilience and a growth mindset.

The Benefits of Embracing Failure
Learning and Growth

- Failure provides valuable lessons that contribute to personal and professional growth. Each mistake teaches you something new.

Resilience and Adaptability

- Experiencing failure helps build resilience and adaptability. It prepares you to handle future challenges with greater ease.

Innovation and Creativity

- Failure often sparks innovation and creativity. When things don't go as planned, you're forced to think outside the box and find new solutions.

Increased Motivation

- Overcoming failure can boost your motivation and determination to succeed. It reinforces your commitment to your goals.

Humility and Empathy

- Failure fosters humility and empathy, helping you relate to others' struggles and offering support.

Contrary to popular belief, failure is not the opposite of success—it's an integral part of the journey towards success. Some of the world's most successful individuals have experienced significant failures. Thomas Edison, who failed thousands of times before inventing the light bulb, famously said, "I have not failed. I've just found 10,000 ways that won't work." His persistence and willingness to learn from failure led to one of the greatest inventions in history. J.K. Rowling was rejected by multiple publishers before Harry Potter became a global phenomenon. Steve Jobs was fired from Apple, the company he co-founded, before returning to lead it to unprecedented success.

Reframing Failure

To embrace failure, it's crucial to shift your perspective:

1. See failure as feedback: Every failure provides valuable information about what doesn't work, bringing you closer to what does.
2. View failure as a learning opportunity: Each setback offers lessons that can improve your approach in the future.

3. Understand that failure is temporary: A single failure does not define your entire journey or worth.
4. Recognize failure as a sign of effort: If you're failing, it means you're trying, which is more valuable than not trying at all.

As author and motivational speaker Denis Waitley puts it, "Failure should be our teacher, not our undertaker. Failure is delay, not defeat. It is a temporary detour, not a dead end."

Strategies for Embracing Failure

Develop a growth mindset
Cultivate the belief that abilities and intelligence can be developed through effort, learning, and persistence. This mindset, coined by psychologist Carol Dweck, allows you to see challenges and failures as opportunities for growth rather than indicators of fixed limitations.

Practice self-compassion
   Be kind to yourself when you fail. Treat yourself with the same compassion you would offer a friend facing a setback. Self-compassion reduces the fear of failure and increases the likelihood of trying again.

Analyze your failures
   After a failure, conduct a thorough, objective analysis:
   - What went wrong?
   - What factors contributed to the failure?
   - What could you have done differently?
   - What lessons can you apply to future attempts?

Celebrate the attempt
Acknowledge the courage it took to try, regardless of the outcome. Thispositivereinforcementcanhelpmaintain motivation for future endeavors.

Share your failures

Discussing your failures with others can provide new perspectives, emotional support, and reduce feelings of isolation. It can also inspire others to persevere through their own challenges.

Set realistic expectations
While ambition is admirable, unrealistic expectations can lead to unnecessary disappointment. Set challenging but achievable goals, and understand that progress often involves small, incremental steps.

Develop resilience
Build your capacity to bounce back from setbacks. This might involve:
- Practicing stress-management techniques
- Maintaining a supportive network
- Focusing on factors within your control
- Cultivating a sense of purpose beyond individual failures

Embrace the "fail fast" mentality
In many fields, particularly entrepreneurship and technology, there's value in failing quickly, learning, and iterating. This approach allows for rapid improvement and innovation.

Keep a failure resume
Alongside your list of successes, maintain a record of your failures and what you learned from each. This can provide perspective and track your growth over time.

Use visualization techniques
Visualize yourself responding positively to failure, learning

from it, and moving forward. This mental rehearsal can help prepare you to handle real-life setbacks more effectively.

Learning from Mistakes: A Step-by-Step Approach

Acknowledge the mistake
Accept that a mistake has been made without judgment or self-criticism.

Take responsibility
Own your part in the mistake, avoiding the temptation to blame others or circumstances.

Reflect on the situation
Consider what led to the mistake and identify any patterns or recurring issues.

Extract lessons
Determine what you can learn from this experience to improve future outcomes.

Develop an action plan
Create specific steps to apply these lessons and prevent similar mistakes.

Implement changes
Put your action plan into practice, monitoring its effectiveness over time.

Share your insights

When appropriate, share what you've learned with others who might benefit from your experience.

Examples of Learning from Failure

Business: Failure in Product Launch
Scenario: A company launches a new product that fails to gain traction in the market.
Learning process:
- Conduct market research to understand why the product didn't resonate
- Gather customer feedback on product features and pricing
- Analyze the marketing strategy and its effectiveness
- Reassess the product development process
- Use insights to improve future product launches or pivot the existing product

Personal: Failed Relationship
Scenario: A long-term relationship ends, leaving one feeling like a failure.
Learning process:
- Reflect on communication patterns and areas for improvement
- Identify personal needs and boundaries for future relationships
- Recognize any recurring issues or red flags that were overlooked
- Seek professional help if needed to process emotions and gain insights
- Use the experience to grow and approach future relation-

ships with new wisdom

Academic: Failing an Important Exam
Scenario: A student fails a crucial exam despite extensive preparation.
Learning process:
- Analyze study techniques and their effectiveness
- Identify gaps in understanding of the material
- Assess time management and stress levels leading up to the exam
- Seek feedback from instructors on areas for improvement
- Develop a new study strategy incorporating these insights for future exams

Overcoming the Fear of Failure

Fear of failure can be paralyzing, preventing people from taking risks and pursuing their goals. To overcome this fear:

Recognize that failure is universal
Everyone fails at some point. Understanding this can reduce the stigma and fear associated with failure.

Start small
Begin with low-stakes situations to build confidence in your ability to handle setbacks.

Redefine success
Broaden your definition of success to include learning and personal growth, not just achieving specific outcomes.

Challenge negative self-talk
When you catch yourself engaging in negative self-talk about failure, consciously replace it with more balanced, constructive thoughts.

Visualize the worst-case scenario
Often, the fear of failure is worse than the reality. Visualizing and planning for the worst-case scenario can make it seem more manageable.

Focus on the process
Shift your focus from the outcome to the process of learning and improvement.

Seek inspiration
Read or listen to stories of successful people who have overcome significant failures.

Practical Exercises to Embrace Failure

Failure Journal

- Keep a journal where you document your failures. Reflect on each experience, noting what you learned and how you can apply those lessons in the future.

Post-Mortem Analysis

- After a project or task, conduct a post-mortem analysis. Identify what went well, what didn't, and what you can do differently next time.

Growth Mindset Affirmations

- Create and repeat affirmations that reinforce a growth mindset, such as "I learn from my mistakes" or "Failure is a stepping stone to success."

Feedback Loop

- Establish a feedback loop where you regularly seek input from mentors, peers, or colleagues. Use this feedback to improve and grow.

Risk-Taking Challenges

- Challenge yourself to take risks and step out of your comfort zone. Embrace the possibility of failure as a part of the process.

Sara Blakely, founder of Spanx, attributes much of her success to her willingness to embrace failure. She keeps a journal of her failures and lessons learned, which has helped her innovate and grow her business.

Michael Jordan, one of the greatest basketball players of all time, famously said, "I've missed more than 9,000 shots in my career. I've lost almost 300 games. Twenty-six times, I've been trusted to take the game-winning shot and missed. I've failed over and over and over again in my life. And that is why I succeed." His willingness to embrace failure contributed to his legendary career.

Practical Exercises to Embrace Failure
Failure Celebration

- Celebrate your failures by acknowledging the effort you put in and the lessons learned. This can shift your mindset to view failure positively.

Failure Support Group

- Join or create a support group where members share their failures and the lessons learned. This can provide encouragement and different perspectives.

Mindfulness Meditation

- Practice mindfulness meditation to reduce anxiety and build resilience. Focus on being present and accepting failure as a natural part of life.

Creative Problem Solving

- Use creative problem-solving techniques, such as brainstorming or mind mapping, to find innovative solutions to challenges and learn from failed attempts.

Visualize Success and Failure

- Spend time visualizing both success and failure. Imagine how you will handle setbacks and use them as learning opportunities.

"Success is not final, failure is not fatal: It is the courage to continue that counts."
– Winston Churchill

Embracing failure and learning from mistakes is a powerful approach to personal and professional growth. By reframing failure as a valuable teacher rather than a final judgment, you open yourself to continuous improvement and resilience.

As author and entrepreneur Seth Godin notes, "The person who fails the most wins." This paradoxical statement encapsulates the idea that those who are willing to fail often—and learn from those failures—are the ones who ultimately succeed.

Remember, every setback carries the seed of an equal or greater benefit. By embracing failure, extracting its lessons, and persisting in the face of challenges, you're not just learning to cope with failure—you're learning to use it as a springboard to success.

Cultivate the courage to fail, the wisdom to learn, and the persistence to try again. In doing so, you'll find that failure is not the end of the road, but rather a vital part of the journey towards achieving your goals and realizing your full potential.

Are you ready to embrace failure and learn from your mistakes?

25

Maintaining Progress: Keep Moving Forward

"Success is the sum of small efforts, repeated day in and day out."
– Robert Collier

Achieving goals and overcoming procrastination is a significant accomplishment, but maintaining progress and continuing to move forward is equally important. This chapter explores strategies to sustain momentum, prevent relapse into old habits, and keep progressing toward your objectives.

The Importance of Sustained Progress

Maintaining progress is crucial for several reasons:

1. Compound effect: Small, consistent efforts accumulate over time, leading to significant results.
2. Habit formation: Consistent progress helps solidify posi-

tive habits.
3. Motivation boost: Seeing continuous improvement fuels further motivation.
4. Resilience building: Steady progress helps you weather setbacks more effectively.

As motivational speaker Zig Ziglar said, "People often say that motivation doesn't last. Well, neither does bathing - that's why we recommend it daily."

Strategies for Maintaining Progress

Set Clear, Measurable Goals
Having well-defined objectives provides direction and allows you to track progress. Use the SMART goal framework:
- Specific
- Measurable
- Achievable
- Relevant
- Time-bound

Example: Instead of "get fit," set a goal like "run a 5K in under 30 minutes within the next 3 months."

Break Large Goals into Smaller Milestones
Divide your main objective into smaller, manageable tasks. This approach:
  - Makes the overall goal less overwhelming
  - Provides frequent opportunities for achievement and motivation
  - Allows for easier tracking of progress

Establish a Routine

Create a structured schedule that incorporates actions towards your goals. Consistency is key to maintaining progress.

Example: If your goal is to write a book, set aside a specific time each day for writing, even if it's just for 30 minutes.

Track Your Progress

Regularly monitor and record your advancements. This can involve:

- Keeping a journal
- Using a progress-tracking app
- Creating a visual representation of your progress (e.g., a progress bar)

Seeing your progress visually can be highly motivating and help you identify areas needing attention.

Celebrate Small Wins

Acknowledge and celebrate your achievements, no matter how small. This positive reinforcement can boost motivation and make the journey more enjoyable.

As author James Clear notes, "Success is a few simple disciplines, practiced every day; while failure is simply a few errors in judgment, repeated every day."

Stay Flexible and Adjust as Needed

Be prepared to adapt your approach based on what you learn along the way. Regularly assess your strategies and be willing to make changes if something isn't working.

Maintain Accountability

Share your goals with others or find an accountability partner. Knowing that someone else is aware of your objectives can provide extra motivation to stay on track.

Continuous Learning

Invest in ongoing education related to your goals. This might involve:
- Reading books or articles
- Attending workshops or seminars
- Seeking mentorship

Continuous learning helps maintain interest and can provide new strategies for progress.

Practice Self-Care

Taking care of your physical and mental health is crucial for sustained progress. Ensure you're:
- Getting enough sleep
- Eating a balanced diet
- Exercising regularly
- Managing stress effectively

Visualize Success

Regularly visualize yourself achieving your goals. This mental practice can reinforce your commitment and boost motivation.

Overcoming Common Obstacles to Progress

Plateaus

It's common to hit plateaus where progress seems to stall. To overcome these:

- Reassess your approach and look for areas to optimize
- Introduce variety to prevent boredom
- Set new, challenging mini-goals to reignite motivation

Burnout
  To avoid burnout:
  - Ensure you're balancing effort with rest
  - Take regular breaks
  - Engage in activities unrelated to your main goal for refreshment

Loss of Motivation
  When motivation wanes:
  - Revisit your 'why'—the reason you set this goal initially
  - Look back at how far you've come
  - Seek inspiration from others who have achieved similar goals

Unexpected Setbacks
  When facing setbacks:
  - View them as temporary and part of the journey
  - Focus on factors within your control
  - Adjust your plan if necessary, but don't give up on the goal

Perfectionism
  Don't let perfectionism hinder your progress:
  - Focus on consistent effort rather than perfect execution
  - Remember that progress is more important than perfection
  As Voltaire said, "Perfect is the enemy of good."

Examples of Maintaining Progress in Different Areas

Fitness Goals
 - Use a fitness tracker to monitor daily activity
 - Join a gym class or running group for accountability
 - Gradually increase workout intensity or duration
 - Try new exercises to prevent boredom

Career Advancement
 - Set quarterly professional development goals
 - Seek regular feedback from supervisors
 - Network consistently, not just when job hunting
 - Keep a log of accomplishments and skills acquired

Learning a New Skill (e.g., Language)
 - Use spaced repetition techniques for vocabulary
 - Practice with native speakers regularly
 - Set progressive goals (e.g., read a children's book, then a newspaper)
 - Immerse yourself through movies, podcasts, or music in the target language

Financial Goals
 - Automate savings and investments
 - Review and adjust your budget monthly
 - Educate yourself continuously about personal finance
 - Celebrate milestones (e.g., paying off a debt, reaching a savings target)

Tools and Techniques for Maintaining Progress

Habit Tracking Apps
Use apps like Habitica, Streaks, or Loop Habit Tracker to monitor daily habits.

Project Management Tools
Utilize tools like Trello or Asana to break down goals and track progress on larger projects.

The Pomodoro Technique
Work in focused 25-minute intervals followed by short breaks to maintain productivity.

Journaling
Maintain a progress journal to reflect on achievements and challenges.

Vision Boards
Create and regularly update a visual representation of your goals to stay inspired.

Jane, a writer, set a goal to write a novel within a year. She broke this down into monthly word count goals and tracked her progress daily. By regularly reviewing her goals and staying flexible with her writing schedule, she maintained steady progress and completed her novel on time.

Mark wanted to develop a habit of reading every day. He started with just 10 minutes of reading each night before bed, stacking this habit onto his existing bedtime routine. Over time, he increased his reading time and now enjoys an hour of reading daily.

Emma, an entrepreneur, faced a setback when her product launch didn't go as planned. Instead of giving up, she analyzed the feedback, adjusted her marketing strategy, and sought advice from her mentor. This approach helped her turn the setback into a valuable learning experience and ultimately led to a successful relaunch.

Alex, a student, used a progress journal to track his study habits and academic achievements. By reviewing his entries weekly and practicing visualization, he maintained consistent study routines and improved his grades significantly.

Maintaining progress is about embracing the journey of continuous improvement. It's not always about dramatic leaps forward, but rather consistent, purposeful steps in the right direction. As author James Clear puts it, "You do not rise to the level of your goals. You fall to the level of your systems."

Remember that progress is rarely linear. There will be ups and downs, rapid advancements and temporary setbacks. The key is to keep moving forward, no matter how small the steps may seem. Each action, each decision, each moment of perseverance builds upon the last, creating a momentum that can carry you towards your goals.

Embrace the process, celebrate your progress, learn from setbacks, and keep pushing forward. As you do, you'll not only achieve your immediate goals but also develop the resilience, discipline, and adaptability that will serve you in all areas of life.

In the words of Martin Luther King Jr., "If you can't fly then run, if you can't run then walk, if you can't walk then crawl, but whatever you do you have to keep moving forward."

Your journey of progress is uniquely yours. Embrace it, nurture it, and keep moving forward. The path may be long, but with consistent effort and the right mindset, you have the power to achieve remarkable things.

Maintaining progress and keeping moving forward requires consistency, resilience, and a positive mindset. By setting short-term goals, tracking your progress, building sustainable habits, overcoming setbacks, and using practical exercises, you can ensure continuous improvement and achieve long-term success. Embrace the journey, celebrate your milestones, and keep striving for your goals.

Are you ready to maintain your progress and keep moving forward?